Eating Disorders

Eating Disorders

Edwina Rogers

To order additional copies of this book, contact:
Xlibris
1-888-795-4274
www.Xlibris.com
Orders@Xlibris.com
748998

Contents

PART I

Overview of Eating Disorders

CHAPTER I

When Food Becomes the Enemy

Katy is a sixteen-year-old girl who was brought to the clinic by her mother. Her mother has a growing concern about her daughter's eating habits, saying she has lost a significant amount of weight in the last few months. Katy has stated several times she is "too fat" and wants to lose weight. Her mother reports she is irritable and constantly shuts down at home, especially when her mother tries to get her to eat more.

Katy's mother said she has noticed her daughter takes careful consideration in the foods she eats, only eating raw vegetables and crackers, drinking lots of water, and refusing to eat what her mom makes for dinner. Although Katy sometimes takes a pastry with her from the house on her way to school, Katy's mother is worried she may not be eating it or anything else the rest of the day. Katy's teachers have reported Katy seems to have low energy at school and often falls asleep in class, whereas in previous years she has been a straight-A student.

Katy's mother has brought her to the doctor because she says Katy passed out at home the day before. Her mother believes it is because Katy is not eating enough to sustain her throughout the day. Katy's mother is worried about her and doesn't know how to help her daughter.

Eating Disorders

It's a familiar story. Eating disorders are a complicated mix of significant weight-related issues. In the United States, approximately 1% to 3% of women are diagnosed with an eating disorder. But the number of young adult women who report engaging in unhealthy eating practices and yet do not meet criteria for eating disorder diagnoses is considerably higher. Sixty-one percent of college women have indicated that they either occasionally or regularly used extreme measures to control their weight, such as fasting, appetite suppressants, diuretics, or purging after eating.

Eating disorders feature serious and obsessive behaviors that are exhibited in extremely inappropriate eating habits due to body image distortion, a need for control in their life, or as a coping mechanism for stress. In the eight distinct eating disorders that are outlined in the DSM-5, some of the symptoms do overlap and most of the resulting health issues are similar but each one exhibits behaviors that are specific to that disorder. All result in seriously negative psychological, physical and social consequences. Often an eating disorder follows drastic attempts to control weight that develop into repeated obsessions or ritualistic behavior that the person feels compelled to perform.

Eating disorders affect people of all ages and both genders, though they are seen 2.5 times more often in females. Often the underlying cause of anxiety and stress begins in childhood. They most often appear in teens but can develop in adults even in older adults. Eating disorders are an expression of mental illness and can be treated. Many times eating disorders coexist with other mental illness, substance abuse and anxiety disorders. Diagnosis is often difficult due to the fact that the symptoms are the same as many other health issues, can be hidden, and require close observation to recognize.

Eating disorders can be life threatening if treatment is not received. Anorexia nervosa is associated with mortality more than any other psychiatric disorder. The research shows that eating disorders are complicated and can result from genetic, biological, psychological, and social factors all interacting together. Brain imaging has allowed medical professionals to study the target areas that are affected by eating disorders. Knowing how the brain functions in connection to such obsessions with food will give clues to better treat such illness.

As in all medical issues, prevention is the ultimate goal. Understanding the progressive effect on the brain can help guide further prevention and treatment efforts. Knowledge of symptoms of the underlying mental illnesses must be a focus in prevention of full blown eating disorders. Having strategies in place, including the education of the public and medical professionals can greatly advance prevention of the eating disorder. Parental awareness of signs and symptoms of such tendencies that appear inappropriate or obsessive must be increased as well.

The Diagnostic and Statistical Manual of Mental Disorders (DSM-5)

While they have been found to have many similarities, there are enough distinctive eating behaviors to warrant their definition in the Diagnostic and Statistical Manual of Mental Disorders (DSM-5) as eight separate yet related disorders:

1. Anorexia Nervosa (AN)
2. Bulimia Nervosa (BN)
3. Avoidant/Restrictive Food Intake Disorder (ARFID)
4. Binge Eating Disorder (BED)
5. Pica
6. Rumination Disorder
7. Other Specified Feeding or Eating Disorder (OSFED)
8. Unspecified Feeding or Eating Disorder (UFED).

The last two, OSFED and UFED, were once combined and referred to as "Eating Disorders Not Otherwise Specified" (EDNOS).

"Other Specified Feeding or Eating Disorder" now refers to some other specific sort of disordered eating, like night eating disorder, or compulsive over-eating, that are not officially recognized and don't yet have agreed upon diagnostic criteria, but nonetheless do occur, and can even be quite common.

"Unspecified Feeding and Eating Disorder" is reserved for instances where there is clearly an eating disorder but it may be quite idiosyncratic or is not (yet) clearly defined or describable.

An emerging disorder, orthorexia nervosa, while not yet clinically recognized, centers around the individual's obsession with what they claim is "healthy" eating.

Causes of Eating Disorders

Eating disorders are complex illnesses that can be triggered by a wide variety of biological and environmental variables. It is important to note that the person with an eating disorder did not wake up one day with this disease. It is created within the person over time as he or she attempts to cope with issues in life that are stressful. And although girls and women are the focus of many eating disorder studies, there are many boys and men who suffer from this disease as well.

Eating disorders include a range of conditions characterized by an intense obsession with food, weight, and appearance. The obsession is often so strong that it disrupts an individual's daily activities, health, social and familial relationships, and career. It is estimated that over ten million people in the United States suffer from eating disorders such as anorexia, bulimia, and binge eating disorder, and the numbers are growing.

Cultural Pressure

Researchers have identified a variety of causal agents. Especially in young women, identification with extreme thinness as a beauty ideal is a well-established predictor of eating disorder symptoms. Ideals for thinness refer both to an individual's awareness of sociocultural pressures to fit a thin prototype and to the internalization of the thinness beauty standard. It is believed that social pressures to conform to the thin body shape ideal have contributed to the increased incidence of eating disorders among young women.

One way to approach the influence of exposure to ideal-looking models in the media on body image is through social comparison theory. First described by social psychologist Leon Festinger (1954), this theory proposes the common-sense notion that people have an innate tendency to compare their attributes, including physical appearance, to others as a method of self-evaluation. Theoretically, media exposure most often produces a negative body image, because when individuals compare their appearance to ideal-looking models, it generally leads to "upward comparison," whereby individuals deem themselves as less attractive than the models.

It must be remembered that most people are repeatedly exposed to body images in the media and the vast majority do not develop eating disorders. Research findings have consistently shown that, as the *internalization* of ideals for thinness increase, so do eating disorder symptoms. More specifically, it is internalization rather than awareness alone that consistently accounts for more of the variance associated with measures of eating disorder symptoms, suggesting that it is the embracing of these ideals, and not just the exposure to them, that is associated with eating disorder symptomatology.

Aside from cultural influences, there are many other factors that may lead an individual to embrace an eating disorder.

Biochemical and Biological Causes

Scientists are researching possible biochemical and biological causes of eating disorders. In some individuals with eating disorders, certain chemicals in the brain that control hunger, appetite, and digestion have been found to be unbalanced. Brain imaging studies have shown that people with eating disorders may have altered brain circuitry that contributes to eating disorders. These differences may help to explain why people who develop anorexia nervosa are able to inhibit their appetite, why people who develop bulimia nervosa have less ability to control impulses to purge, and why people who develop binge eating disorder are vulnerable to overeating when they are hungry.

Genetics

Eating disorders often run in families. Current research indicates that there may be significant genetic contributions to eating disorders. Increasing numbers of family, twin, and adoption research studies have provided compelling evidence to show that genetic factors contribute to a predisposition for eating disorders. This suggests that individuals who are born with certain genotypes are at heightened risk for the development of an eating disorder.

Trauma and Psychological Issues

Psychological causes of an eating disorder may include low self-esteem, feelings of inadequacy or lack of control in life, depression, anxiety, anger, stress, or loneliness.

Interpersonal issues may include a history of physical or sexual abuse, troubled personal relationships, difficulty expressing emotions and feelings, or a history of being teased or ridiculed based on size or weight.

Traumatic events such as physical or sexual abuse sometimes precipitate the development of an eating disorder. Eating disorders can become a mechanism with which to cope with rape, incest, and other trauma. Survivors of trauma often struggle with shame, guilt, body dissatisfaction and a feeling of a lack of control, and eating disorders are common for adult survivors of childhood sexual abuse and for survivors of sexual assaults as adults. The eating disorder may emerge as a distorted expression of self-medication or misdirected self-punishment for the trauma. It can thus be seen as the individual's attempt to regain control or cope with these intense emotions.

For some survivors of sexual abuse, developing an eating disorder is a way to avoid sexuality and its painful memories. In stressful events like rape or molestation, the victim often feels that their control over their own body has been taken, and may seek extreme ways to increase their sense of control. In other cases, an eating disorder may be a way to hide anger or frustration and seek the approval of other people.

Common Traits in Eating Disorders

Even a partial eating disorder that has not been diagnosed or classified can be dangerous and lead to death. Family and friends often see the problem as something other than an eating disorder. And even though eating disorders may each have different pathologies, they often share three things in common:

1.   A recurring inappropriate behavior.
2.   The fear of changing their habits.
3.   Denial that the problem is serious.

In unspecified eating disorders the binge eating and purging may occur less frequently than in the classic type, or an individual might maintain a normal weight and still have bouts of anorexic behaviors.

Eating disorders are similar to all addictive behaviors and often occur at the same time. They are all coping behaviors to deal with stress and to manage emotional regulation.

Eating Disorders and Behavioral Addictions

In all addicts of any kind, the brain changes to rely on the coping mechanisms that are unhealthy to the body. The changes can actually be seen in brain imaging. Though eating disorders are similar to addictive behavior, research has revealed eating disorders are set in place during childhood, which make them difficult to treat where most other addictions are developed later, during teen and adult years.

Research also shows the effect of sports on eating disorders. Many sports require weight limits. And, supported by a coach or peers, a young person learns specific methods for dropping and gaining weight. Their desire to achieve and improve becomes tied into control of food and working out. Often obsessive exercise is a by-product of sports along with eating disorders.

Adaptive Functions and Rituals

Having friends and activities that help us to feel calm is healthy and normal, but when a person begins to overcompensate for negative feelings with one unhealthy activity, like smoking, to relieve stress, they are using what has been called an adaptive function. These adapted actions are temporary fixes and only give the good feeling of calm while the behavior continues. Sometimes the behaviors become rituals that are acted upon repeatedly, or even obsessively. The brain is unable to feel good with more appropriate support of friends and healthy desires. Research has consistently found a correlation between anxiety and stress and eating disorders. Most patients with eating disorders began the downhill slide into cyclical and compulsive unhealthy behaviors due to anxiety that overwhelmed them. This ritualistic behavior can be seen in young children who compulsively approach situations that cause them stress, like pushing chairs up to the table whenever they are slightly pulled back, or having to stack and restack their books or picking at things, and even pulling out hair. Some perform rituals that consist of saying something over and over, having unusual fears if they don't get the ritual right, and dreading any changes in those rituals.

Categorical Vs. Dimensional Analysis

It has been proposed that eating disorders should be placed on a continuum as opposed to specific categories, as one type might lead to another. This is called dimensional, rather than categorical, diagnosis. For example, one dimension might be "over-controlled eating" (like anorexia) versus "under-controlled eating" (like binge eating disorder), while another dimension might include something like "distorted body image" vs. "accurate body image."

According to this "dimensional analysis," individuals might be ordered along some set of such dimensions instead of being categorized according to a taxonomy of different disorders. A dimensional diagnosis would offer the tandem advantages of having no one slip through the cracks, because everyone would appear somewhere on the dimensions, and no two people would occupy exactly the same place along the various dimensions, rather than having a set of people all diagnosed as "bulimic" but having varying types and severity of symptoms.

However, because treatment is specific to the type of disorder, and the behaviors exhibited by each type are different, the use of a categorical approach to the diagnosis of eating disorders has been retained in the DSM-5.

Effects on Physical and Psychological Health

Eating disorders are considered mental disorders that interfere with physical and psychological health because of a person's obsession with body image or weight. They are not the same as dieting or having alternative eating habits. Eating disorders have an underlying cause that results in compulsive, restrictive, and addictive forms of eating. They can result in poor physical health, sometimes even causing organ failure. In fact, due to malnutrition the organs in a person with an eating disorder can shut down before a person becomes exceedingly underweight.

Eating disorders develop because an individual struggles with emotional control or personal conflict. Just like the fear of water has nothing to do with the water itself, the disordered eating may have little to do with food. It is a response to overwhelming distress and the notion that slimness will solve an emotional problem. Society promotes a perfect body image, losing weight, and a distorted idea of what is healthy until we are brainwashed to think that good things come only to the thin. Young women and teens are the most likely to fall prey to such ideas because such messages often target them, and their emotional states are so connected with what their peers think of them.

Shame and Stigma

As medical and psychological sciences continue to learn about the various mental illnesses that affect humans and that often begin at an early stage where the foundation for a need of coping mechanisms is learned, the need for education about such mental illness increases. Like the eating disorder itself, the compensation for the eating disorder also appears gradually. The gap between medical science and the general population in understanding and observation of symptoms and causes is huge.

Parents don't want to consider their child as having any disorder and mental disorders continue to be kept hidden and private within families. People don't want to think anyone in their own family is not "normal."

For the individual themselves, they often don't recognize that what they do as being inappropriate. Many times they have friends who do the same thing and possibly introduce the person to such behaviors. For any individual to succumb to such obsessive compensations for eating requires an underlying inability to cope with stress.

How the individual perceives themselves can vary greatly with the specific disorder. For example, anorexia is characterized by a perverse sense of discipline, restraint, and self-sacrifice—traits that society ordinarily upholds as virtuous. The anorexic may feel not shame but pride in their dubious accomplishment. In contrast, bulimia is characterized by a consuming and corrosive sense of shame. The bulimic knows that there is nothing respectable about gorging yourself past the point of physical discomfort before thrusting your fingers in your mouth to induce vomiting. Habitually hiding your self-destructive behavior from others can lead to deep personal shame.

Treatment Options

Eating disorders can become chronic, debilitating, and even life-threatening conditions. According to the National Institute of Mental Health, sufferers of anorexia are eighteen times more likely to die prematurely, so getting treatment for an eating disorder is extremely important.

Early diagnosis and intervention may enhance recovery. While no simple cure exists for eating disorders, treatment is available and recovery is possible. Treatments for various eating disorders are similar in that they involve cognitive-behavioral therapy, interpersonal therapy, and antidepressant medication, in addition to other forms of intervention aimed at enhancing emotional regulation, relaxation, stress management, and body awareness. Psychological counseling must address both the eating-disordered symptoms and the underlying psychological, interpersonal, and cultural forces that are contributing to the eating disorder.

Generally, the goals of eating disorder treatment are to help the individual attain a healthy weight, treat any psychological problems related to the disorder, and reduce behaviors or thoughts that contribute to the eating disorder. The exact treatment needs of each individual will vary. Many people with eating disorders respond to outpatient therapy, including individual, group, or family therapy, and medical management by their primary care provider. Support groups, nutritional counseling, and psychiatric medications under careful medical supervision have also proven helpful for some individuals.

At the start of treatment patients that are extremely underweight or have other medical complications, so medical attention may be the first and most important step to get the person to a healthy weight and to treat any serious medical problems.

When an eating disorder has led to physical problems that may be life threatening, or when it is associated with severe psychological or behavioral problems, hospital-based care (including inpatient, partial hospitalization, intensive outpatient and/or residential care in an eating disorders specialty unit or facility) is necessary.

An effective treatment strategy is a multimodal team-based approach. This treatment method involves the contributions of a team of professionals including a medical doctor, nutritionist, therapist, and a psychiatrist for medication management. Psychotherapy is important in treating any associated mental disorders, such as depression or anxiety that may be contributing to the eating disorder. Nutritional counseling is an important part of recovery and long-term success.

Cognitive behavioral therapy (CBT) is often a component of eating disorder treatment. This structured therapy is done in sessions, either individually, in a group, or with family. Cognitive behavioral therapy is goal-oriented and focuses on changing unhealthy thought patterns, producing positive changes in behavior. Considered the treatment of choice for eating disorders, CBT is frequently combined with other treatment options.

Any treatment should be tailored to the individual and needs to vary according to both the severities of the disorder and the patient's particular problems, needs, and strengths.

CHAPTER 2

Types of Eating Disorders, Part 1

*A*ngel, a seventeen-year-old high school junior, had always felt she was overweight, even since early childhood. Angel first noticed she began paying more attention to her weight during middle school. She noted this period of her life as being particularly stressful. She constantly worried her parents might divorce because they argued daily. In addition, Angel began attending a new school where she did not know any of the children and had few friends. Many of the "popular" girls in school began picking on her, pinching her rear end and calling her "chubby." Angel recalled many of the girls would change clothes for gym in the locker room together, but she always changed in one of the stalls because she worried the other girls would make comments about the way she looked.

Angel also noted her mother was overweight and was "always on some kind of diet." When Angel began the sixth grade, her mother signed up for Weight Watchers and signed up Angel, too. Angel recalled the Weight Watchers meetings as being somewhat informative, but then she, her mother and her aunt would all go to a restaurant afterwards where they would proceed to eat to the point of feeling sick. Angel also noted that while on Weight Watchers her mother would often prepare her tuna sandwiches to take for lunch. Angel remembers having to eat the tuna sandwiches while the other children enjoyed their own trays of food. They would ask Angel, "Why are you eating that?" She felt ashamed and embarrassed.

At the beginning of high school and after years of frustration with her weight and body, Angel made the decision that she would "just stop eating altogether." She *would skip breakfast and lunch while at school and then come home and eat a tomato sandwich for dinner "so my parents wouldn't know." Angel lost a significant amount of weight in a very short period of time. She confessed she was happy with her progress and it motivated her to continue her destructive eating patterns.*

However, she also began to experience many negative side effects. Angel took notice that she was tired all of the time and her skin looked pale. She began passing out when she would stand up too fast. Angel recalled one time when she climbed out of the bathtub she passed out and thought she had experienced a seizure. She said she never told her parents.

Angel admitted to being "a bit" concerned about her eating habits and her health, but acknowledged she is more fearful of gaining weight. Regarding vomiting or taking laxatives, Angel admitted engaging in these behaviors has "crossed her mind," but she has never done so. She expressed concern that she may not be able to eat normally again and became tearful at the thought of having to eat her "fear foods" such as mashed potatoes and white bread. Angel has sought help from a professional to assist with these issues.

Anorexia Nervosa (AN)

The most common eating disorder is anorexia nervosa (AN), which means "a nervous loss of appetite," and it is one of the most difficult eating disorders to diagnose, especially in growing female teens. Because growth can happen in spurts, it is often difficult to attribute the excessive thinness to an eating disorder instead of growing taller in a short time span. Often it takes time to figure out the signs. A typical anorectic (the noun of the disease anorexia) will be rigid in routines, appear to be a perfectionist, and have a low self-esteem.

A sudden weight loss might not be a warning sign. Doctors may instead look for a lack of sufficient nutrients being consumed to meet the needs of the body, and disturbed or distorted body image perceptions (i.e., thinking they are "fat" when, in fact, they are emaciated).

No longer is there a requirement of lack of regular menstrual cycles because research has shown that some patient's cycles do not end and because that behavior excludes males and pre-pubescent girls.

Anorectics can disguise eating by pushing food around on the plate, chewing and spitting it into a napkin or moving into purging and bulimia. They can feel extreme guilt after eating and then punish themselves when hunger pains are felt by refusing to eat. Drinking a lot of water, chewing gum, and taking part in extended exercise are other ways devised to detract the brain from the sensation of hunger.

Isolation of the individual often develops because of the need to control their eating habits, loss of enjoyment in social activities, and the need for tight routines. The more isolated the person becomes the more control is exercised in order to avoid negative feelings.

Feelings about body image, obesity, and any other problem can start with choosing to diet using unhealthy and uninformed methods and progress into habitual obsessive eating habits. Unhealthy diets open a person to physical and mental illness. The difference between an eating disorder and disordered eating is the extent that it controls everything a person does in life.

Anorexia nervosa does not have the requirement of any specific amount of time spent in such activity or to any such degree, in order to be diagnosed. Physicians look for disordered patterns of eating on a regular basis that appear as addiction and it is often treated as a behavioral addiction.

Anorexia nervosa can have multiple complications. At its most serious, it can be fatal. Death may occur suddenly, even when the person is not yet severely underweight. This may result from abnormal heart rhythms (arrhythmias) or an imbalance of electrolytes—minerals such as calcium, potassium, and sodium that maintain the balance of fluids in the body.

The Two Types of Anorexia Nervosa (AN)

It was in the research and writings of William Gull and his report about a fourteen-year-old girl that the term "anorexia nervosa" was used and that brought the disorder to the forefront. He and Earnest-Charles Lasegue first defined the disorder with a list of symptoms in 1873. Over the years such symptoms have been more defined and with new classifications introduced.

There are two subcategories of anorexia nervosa.

Anorexia nervosa restricting (ANR) can present as a restriction to eating only one food or a small group of foods or to merely drinking water, coffee, or tea.

Anorexia nervosa binge-eating/purging type (ANBP) may seem to fit more with bulimia nervosa in how the symptoms and underlying need for control fit the diagnosis, binge-eating and purging is often an impulsive, loss of control action and must be treated as such.

Anorexia Nervosa and Anxiety

Recent studies show that individuals who suffer from anorexia nervosa often demonstrate exaggerated anxiety related to food and eating. There is often an increased level of intolerance of uncertainty or worry, inhibition and inflexibility before eating that can lead to avoidant or compensatory behaviors. Confronting food or anticipating eating creates anxiety as opposed what for most people is a pleasant experience. The anxiety is exaggerated to the point that even the anticipation of eating will bring on feelings of depression.

This exaggerated response seems to be a general characteristic that is present in other contexts, as well. Bischoff-Grethe, et al., reported that brain imaging of individuals suffering from anorexia nervosa also showed exaggerated responses after loses and normal responses after wins. They also found a higher sensitivity to punishment and lower to reward activity. The preoccupation with the anticipated negative consequences of eating overpowered any positive feelings of a reward for eating. The brain imaging also showed a hypersensitivity to criticism.

After eating, the anorectic individual has powerful feelings of degradation and self-loathing and then must cope with those feelings.

In light of these neurobiological findings from research in brain imaging, treatment for anorexia nervosa now incorporates a focus on the anxiety in order to correct the coping strategy of avoidance.

Symptoms

While the outward physical symptoms of anorexia nervosa are related to starvation, the disorder also includes significant behavioral and emotional issues related to a distorted perception of body weight and an extremely strong fear of gaining weight or becoming fat.

A. Physical signs and symptoms of anorexia may include hair loss, brittle nails, dry and yellowish skin, loss of lanugo (the fine soft hair that covers the body), muscle and bone weakness and deterioration, tooth loss, heart muscle wasting, anemia, swollen joints, constipation, insomnia, infertility, organ failure, coma and death. Anorectics also have lower body temperatures, and the fat cells shrink causing loss of appetite. Ironically, as the body goes into a state of starvation, ketones are produced and have a very similar structure to another brain chemical that has an analgesic affect upon the brain and can lift the person's mood.

B. Emotional and behavioral symptoms may include attempts to lose weight by either severely restricting food intake through dieting or fasting, excessive exercise, and self-induced vomiting to get rid of the food. Self-medication may include use of laxatives, enemas, diet aids, or herbal products.

The person may also have an intense preoccupation with food, a refusal to eat, fear of gaining weight, social withdrawal, lying about how much food has been eaten, reduced interest in sex, and thoughts of death or suicide.

Diagnostic Criteria

It may be difficult to diagnose anorexia because people with the condition often disguise their thinness, eating habits, or physical problems. A diagnosis may be based on these criteria. The DSM-5 diagnosis anorexia in relation to three critical elements:

A. Restriction of energy intake relative to requirements, leading to a significantly low body weight in the context of age sex developmental trajectory, and physical health. Significantly low weight is defined as a weight that is less than minimally normal or, for children and adolescents, less than that minimally expected.

B. Intense fear of gaining weight or of becoming fat, or persistent behavior that interferes with weight gain, even though at a significantly low weight.

C. Disturbance in the way in which one's body weight or shape is experienced, undue influence of body weight or shape on self-evaluation, or persistent lack of recognition of the seriousness of the current low body weight.

Treatment

One of the special challenges of treating anorexia is that the patient may deny they have a problem and may refuse treatment. Barriers to treatment may include thinking they don't need treatment, fearing weight gain, and not seeing anorexia as a disease but rather a lifestyle choice.

Additionally, as The Lancet reported, clinical trials for anorexia nervosa are difficult to conduct, partly because of the challenging task of offering a treatment designed to remove symptoms that patients desperately cling to, the fairly low prevalence of the disorder, and high dropout rates.

Bulimia Nervosa (BN)

Sandra is a fifteen-year-old freshman in high school. Before the school year began, Sandra enjoyed the summer with her first boyfriend. However, he broke up with her just before school started. Sandra heard rumor he had broken up with her because she was too fat, and she also heard he had a new girlfriend at another school who was a cheerleader.

Sandra's best friend, Chelsea, became more and more concerned about Sandra. Chelsea decided to reach out to the school counselor. Chelsea reported she had noticed Sandra was skipping lunch most days, and when she did eat, she made an excuse to go to the bathroom directly after. Chelsea said she also noticed Sandra had become very thin. She tried to talk to Sandra, but Sandra became very defensive, claiming, "There's nothing wrong! I just don't like what they're serving!" Chelsea said Sandra also kept making excuses about why she couldn't go out to social events with Chelsea, claiming she had homework. Chelsea thought she didn't want to go so that Sandra didn't have to worry about being put in a situation where there was food.

The counselor discussed the concerns with Sandra, noting that others were concerned about her eating behaviors. Sandra became very defensive and exclaimed, "I don't like the food they serve here. It's too fattening!" The counselor continued discussing presenting concerns and mentioned Sandra's weight loss and her defensiveness regarding the issue. Eventually Sandra agreed to allow the counselor to call her mother so they could discuss the possibility of additional help.

The person with bulimia nervosa (BN) eats large amounts of food in a short time period or simply loses control during an episode of eating, and then attempts to compensate for that increased caloric intake, typically by purging through forced vomiting, use of laxatives, fasting, and/or excessive exercising.

Bulimia nervosa differs from anorexic binge-purging in that the bulimic individual will purge not for the purpose of becoming thin but to relieve physical and psychological effects of over eating. In the DSM-5, a diagnosis of bulimia nervosa requires a recurrence of an average of at least one binge per week over a three-month period of time. A person suffering from bulimia nervosa is not necessarily thin and does not necessarily exhibit the behavior on a daily basis.

On the other hand, the person with bulimia nervosa is not the person who merely overeats on holidays. Rather, he or she is constantly obsessed with body image and often experiences depression, guilt and self-loathing associated with the uncontrollable cycles of bingeing and purging.

For a bulimic, food is like a drug. Favorite foods and comfort foods which fuel the need for good feelings are often collected and stored in secret places until the bulimic can spend several hours eating and purging, often repeatedly. The feeling of relief and satisfaction the food brings will hold the bulimic until he or she again becomes depressed and anxious and requires substantial amounts of food to again restore emotional calm, which is why many people view bulimia as a dysfunctional approach to emotional regulation. A person who copes with emotional distress by overeating on a regular basis may well be bulimic. Eating food is a normal thing, and often friends and colleagues aren't around others long enough for them to notice the amounts of food a bulimic will consume. Chronic dieting without success is a common precursor to bulimia. Some bulimics are former anorectics and many have low leptin levels, which send messages to the brain that they are not hungry.

Symptoms

In early stages of bulimia, there is less malnutrition and it is characterized by other behavior. Included in the symptoms of bulimia can be a sore throat, swollen salivary glands, eczema, rosacea (reddening of the skin), and bruised knuckles from putting fingers down the throat to induce vomitting, using the bathroom immediately after eating on a regular basis, overeating or undereating, fatigue, irritability, and depression. Severe or long-term bulimics will have tooth erosion, gum disease, inflamed esophagus, acid reflux disorder, anemia, dehydration, heart palpitations, and electrolyte imbalance. Often it is disguised as diabetes.

Diagnostic Criteria

A. The DSM-5 diagnoses bulimia on the basis of the following. First, the individual has to exhibit the following behaviors:

1. Eating, in a discrete period of time (e.g., within any two-hour period), an amount of food that is definitely larger than what most individuals would eat in a similar period of time under similar circumstances.
2. A sense of lack of control over eating during the episode (e.g., a feeling that one cannot stop eating or control what or how much one is eating).

B. Recurrent inappropriate compensatory behaviors in order to prevent weight gain, such as self-induced vomiting; misuse of laxatives, diuretics, or other medications; fasting; or excessive exercise.

C. The binge eating and inappropriate compensatory behaviors both occur, on average, at least once a week for at least three months.

D. Self-evaluation is unduly influenced by body shape and weight.

E. The disturbance does not occur exclusively during episodes of anorexia nervosa.

Treatment

A combination of psychotherapy with antidepressants is often the most effective approach for overcoming the disorder. Psychotherapy, also known as talk therapy or psychological counseling, involves discussing the bulimia and related issues with a mental health provider. Types of psychotherapy that can help improve symptoms of bulimia may include cognitive behavioral therapy, family-based therapy, and interpersonal psychotherapy, among others.

Antidepressants may help reduce the symptoms of bulimia when used along with psychotherapy.

Avoidant/Restrictive Feed Intake Disorder (ARFID)

Avoidant/restrictive food intake disorder (ARFID) is the obsessive need to restrict the diet to a limited array of specific foods. It may actually begin with health in mind as a person plans to eat less meat or become a vegetarian, but the need to control can intensify until the options are severely limited.

ARFID is often confused with anorexia nervosa because weight loss and nutritional deficiency are common shared symptoms. However, the primary difference between ARFID and anorexia is that the person exhibiting ARFID lacks the obsessive desire for thinness, and often has an intense dislike of certain food characteristics, such as texture, taste, consistency or form.

While ARFID affects both genders and is more common in children and young adolescents, it can occur in late adolescence and adulthood as well. ARFID is often associated with a higher levels of psychiatric co-morbidity, especially anxiety and obsessive compulsive disorder.

In children, extreme food refusal, rigid, limited and perseverative eating behaviors may be associated with developmental disabilities, such as Autism Spectrum Disorder. Children may insist upon eating a very limited range of foods that may share similar characteristics such as texture, color, smell or temperature. In older children and adolescents, food avoidance or refusal may be associated with medical conditions such as gastroesophageal reflux or psychological conditions such as trauma, mood disorders, and anxiety disorders. ARFRID is not diagnosed when it is due to medical conditions or is associated with other disorders which may better account for it, like Autism.

Symptoms and Diagnostic Criteria

The DSM-5 diagnosis Avoidant-Restrictive Food Intake Disorder (ARFID) under the following conditions:

A. An eating or feeding disturbance (e.g., apparent lack of interest in eating or food; avoidance based on the sensory characteristics of food; concern about aversive consequences of eating) as manifested by persistent failure to meet appropriate nutritional and/or energy needs associated with one (or more) of the following:

1. Significant weight loss, or, in children, failure to achieve expected weight gain or faltering growth.
2. Significant nutritional deficiency.
3. Dependence on enteral feeding or oral nutritional supplements.
4. Marked interference with psychosocial functioning.

B. The disturbance is not better explained by lack of available food or by an associated culturally sanctioned practice.

C. The eating disturbance does not occur exclusively during the course of anorexia nervosa or bulimia nervosa, and there is no evidence of disturbance in the way in which one's body weight or shape is experienced.

D. The eating disturbance is not attributable to a concurrent medical condition or not better explained by another mental disorder.

Treatment

As Lindsay Kenney, BA and B. Timothy Walsh, MD wrote in *Eating Disorders Review*, little is currently known about effective treatment interventions for individuals presenting with ARFID. However, given the prominent avoidance behaviors, it seems likely that behavioral interventions, such as forms of exposure therapy, may well play an important therapeutic role. For someone with an emotional disturbance such as depression or anxiety that affects feeding (such as in FAED), cognitive behavioral therapy and other treatments for the underlying condition may be an effective approach for treatment of the eating disorder.

Re-feeding in a hospital setting may be a necessary first step in treatment. Often intervention is multidisciplinary approach of occupational, speech, behavioral, and family therapists who work together to establish structured eating patterns and gradually increase food variety. Anxiety management strategies, cognitive restructuring and systematic behavioral exposure are possible interventions for these complex conditions.

CHAPTER 3

Types of Eating Disorders, Part 2

*C*rystal, age twenty-five, has never had any problems in the past with managing her weight. She was active in sports during high school and played softball and golf in college. After college, Crystal was able to find a nursing job fairly quickly. Along with a new job, Crystal also made another important change in her life. She married her college sweetheart, and within one year she became pregnant with their first child. She had a healthy pregnancy and she and her husband were excited to deliver a healthy baby. After the birth of her son, Crystal vowed she wanted to get back in shape and "drop the baby weight." She felt motivated and decided that once she was off of maternity leave and back to work, she would also sign up for a gym membership.

Crystal returned to work, but discovered while she was away during maternity leave her former boss had resigned, and Crystal found herself working under new management. The new boss was very demanding, often requesting the healthcare staff to overbook patients. Crystal noticed he would spend too long with some patients, putting the entire day and other patients behind schedule. The new boss would often take frustrations out on Crystal and sometimes Crystal and the other staff would have to stay later than planned to make sure all the patients for the day were seen.

During this same timeframe, her husband also accepted a new job that required him to work the night shift. Most days he would have to depart the household as soon as Crystal arrived home, leaving her with all the responsibilities of caring for their son, the household and evening meals alone. With the added stress at work and all *the responsibilities at home left for her to do in the evenings, Crystal had less and less time to take care of herself. She became stressed and was exhausted, sometimes too tired to fall asleep at night. Crystal would lie down in bed around 11 p.m. and would toss and turn for up to an hour. Most nights she could only count about four hours of sleep.*

One night after she had finally fallen asleep, she found herself startled awake. Sitting up in bed, she gasped for air, felt her throat and chest tightening, making it difficult to breathe. She jumped out of bed and ran to the kitchen, pouring herself a glass of water. Shaken from the episode, she sat in the kitchen for several minutes trying to calm down and wondered what was wrong with her. She was home alone and worried that if she had not stopped choking when she did, she might have died in her bed, leaving her son home alone with no one to care for him. Panicked by the thought, she tried to soothe herself and went to the fridge to get something to eat. After snacking for a few minutes, she felt herself beginning to calm down and when she felt full, she returned to bed.

Since the first episode that night, Crystal reported she has experienced similar bouts of panic in the night several times. She noticed the only thing that seemed to make her feel better was eating something and attaining a full, soothing feeling. She related the feeling of fullness to feeling "comfortable" and "safe." Crystal became more concerned that the extra calories she has consumed during these episodes were contributing to her weight gain and hindering her progress.

In addition, she became worried her husband might judge her for these episodes. The couple of nights each week that he has been home, she has made excuses to get out of bed, telling her husband she wanted to check on their son. Instead, she found herself in the kitchen snacking on items like ice cream, cookies or chips. One night she guiltily recalled she had eaten half of a pie she had baked earlier in the day. When her husband asked her what had happened to the pie, she told him part of it burned, so she had thrown it out. The additional weight led her to feeling depressed and as if she were a "failure." She experienced guilt about her middle-of-the-night eating habits and worried her husband would think she is unattractive. Frustrated and concerned with her eating patterns, she decided to seek help from a professional counselor.

Binge Eating Disorder (BED)

Binge eating disorder (BED) is often called a food addiction. As with many eating disorders, BED often follows yo-yo dieting. In BED, the person does not compensate in any way for eating. These individuals tend to become increasingly overweight. The DSM-5 lists symptoms as binging that occurs repeatedly (at least one per week on average over the course of at least three months), accompanied by a feeling of being out of control.

A binge eater often consumes between five thousand and fifteen thousand calories in a single sitting, often "gorging" rapidly and ingesting massive quantities of food within a very short period of time. They may also eat every meal each day plus snacks between meals.. The binge episodes are commonly associated with feelings of guilt, remorse, or self-loathing. Unlike bulimia, the individual does not engage in any compensatory behaviors such as self-induced vomiting, use of diuretics, or excessive exercise. For that reason they are often overweight, in contrast to bulimics, who are more commonly average weight.

Binge eating disorder is often seen first during childhood or adolescence and can be associated with health risks. Individuals become extremely obese and can develop asthma, diabetes, insulin rejection, heart trouble, gallstones, a fatty liver, high blood pressure, high cholesterol, joint deterioration, and sleep apnea.

Binge eating disorder often results in many of the same health risks associated with clinical obesity. Additional health consequences of binge eating disorder can include high blood pressure, high cholesterol levels, heart disease as a result of elevated triglyceride levels, type II diabetes mellitus, and gallbladder disease. Physical discomfort and gastrointestinal distress frequently occur due to the high volume of food ingested. The person may experience lethargy and fatigue.

Binge Eating Disorder: Types and Co-morbidity

BED is the most recently recognized eating disorder, having been included for the first time in the 5th Edition of the Diagnostic and Statistical Manual (2013; DSM-5). As with other eating disorders, binge eating is often accompanied by mood disorders, depression, fatigue, anxiety, phobias, and panic attacks. Research points toward restricted diets that cause anxiety that ultimately result in binging. Although they are not officially recognized as diagnostic subtypes, there are two significant variations of binge eating disorder:

1.   Deprivation-sensitive BED.
2.   Dissociative-addictive BED.

Deprivation-sensitive BED comes after the restrictive dieting, whereas with dissociative-addictive BED, the individual has learned to use food as coping method or soothing technique in response to painful emotions. This kind of binging is not episodic but becomes a regularly occurring part of the person's daily behavior, and often begins early in life.

Symptoms and Diagnostic Criteria

A. Recurrent episodes of binge eating. In the DSM-5 binges are characterized by both of the following:

   1. Eating, in a discrete period of time (e.g., within any two-hour period), an amount of food that is definitely larger than what most individuals would eat in a similar period of time under similar circumstances.
   2. A sense of lack of control over eating during the episode (e.g., a feeling that one cannot stop eating or control what or how much one is eating).

In addition:

B. The binge eating episodes are associated with three (or more) of the following:

   1. Eating much more rapidly than normal.
   2. Eating until feeling uncomfortably full.
   3. Eating large amounts of food when not feeling physically hungry.
   4. Eating alone because of feeling embarrassed by how much one is eating.
   5. Feeling disgusted with oneself, depressed, or very guilty afterward.

C. Marked distress regarding binge eating is present.

D. The binge eating occurs, on average, at least once a week for three months.

E. The binge eating is not associated with the recurrent use of inappropriate compensatory behavior as in bulimia nervosa and does not occur exclusively during the course of bulimia nervosa or anorexia nervosa.

Treatment

Professional support and treatment from health professionals specializing in the treatment of binge eating disorders, including psychologists, psychiatrists, nutritionists, clinical social workers and professional counselors, can be the most effective way to address binge eating disorder. Because binge eating is so entwined with feelings of personal shame, poor self-image, and other negative emotions, treatment also may address these and other psychological issues. Binge eating disorder is most commonly treated in an outpatient setting, but residential programs can be powerful tools for those needing extra support and intervention.

Meditation may be effective as a treatment for binge eating. As Jean L. Kristeller and C. Brendan Hallett wrote in 1999, meditation has a long history of being used within spiritual practice, and more recently it has been used for treatment of anxiety, addictions, pain management, and as an adjunct to psychotherapy. Meditation appears to have the potential to facilitate self-regulation, and may enhance insight and the integration of physiological, emotional, cognitive, and behavioral aspects of human functioning.

While there have been anecdotal reports of the value of meditation for treating eating disorders, the effects have not been systematically studied. However, research on meditation suggests it may be effective in addressing many of the factors relevant to binge eating disorder. Individuals with BED appear to suffer from the dysregulation of multiple psychological processes that contribute to binge eating, including elevated anxiety and dysphoria, distorted and reactive thinking patterns, and disturbed awareness of normal physiological cues related to food intake.

Meditation techniques may modify the dysregulated processes associated with BED in several ways. As a way of improving self-acceptance, it may decrease the relative appeal of binge eating as an escape mechanism and facilitate general therapeutic change.

After a binge, it is only natural for the individual to feel the need to diet to compensate for overeating and to get back on track with their health. But dieting usually backfires because the deprivation and hunger that comes with strict dieting triggers food cravings and the urge to overeat. Instead of dieting, as a part of professional counseling individuals are encouraged to focus on eating regularly in moderation.

Pica: Consumption of Non-Food Items

Pica is the consumption, on a regular basis, of non-food items. And though it is common for toddlers to put things in their mouths and even eat non-food items at times, pica is different. Individuals with pica have cravings for specific items and frequently eat many. Some of the things eaten by those with this disease include but are not limited to dirt; chalk; paint chips; cigarette ashes; plaster; feces; ice; glue; hair; buttons; soap; and paper. Though many of the items consumed may not be harmful, pica can indicate a serious mental illness and the ingestion of these things over time can cause major health issues.

Symptoms

The clinical presentation of pica is highly variable and is associated with the specific nature of the ingested substances and the resulting medical conditions. In cases of exposure to infectious agents or poisoning, the reported symptoms are related to the type of toxin or infectious agent ingested. Physical findings may include manifestations of toxic ingestion (such as lead poisoning), infection or parasitic infestation, mechanical bowel problems, constipation, ulcerations, perforations, and intestinal obstructions.

There may be dental manifestations too, including severe tooth abrasion, abfraction, and surface tooth loss.

Diagnostic Criteria

A. Persistent eating of nonnutritive, nonfood substances over a period of at least one month.

B. The eating of nonnutritive, nonfood substances that is inappropriate to the developmental level of the individual.

C. The eating behavior is not part of a culturally supported or socially normative practice.

D. If the eating behavior occurs in the context of another mental disorder (e.g., intellectual disability, autism spectrum disorder, schizophrenia) or medical condition (including pregnancy), it is sufficiently sever to warrant additional clinical attention.

Treatment

No medical treatment is specific for pica. A multidisciplinary approach involving psychologists, social workers, and physicians is recommended for effective treatment.

Behavioral strategies may be effective in the treatment of pica. Some evidence suggests that drugs that enhance dopaminergic functioning, such as olanzapine, may provide treatment alternatives in individuals with pica that is refractory to behavioral intervention.

Rumination Disorder

Rumination disorder is another less common eating disorder. The symptoms are regurgitating food, re-chewing it, and re-swallowing it. It may cause failure to thrive, lowered resistance to disease, and malnutrition. It can also cause irritation of the esophagus due to acids from the stomach. According to the DSM-5, it is only diagnosed as an eating disorder if it is repeated over the course of at least one month, the condition is not associated with gastrointestinal or other medical condition, happens separate from other eating disorders, and it occurs along with another mental illness such as generalized anxiety disorder (GAD) or neurodevelopmental disorder.

Symptoms and Diagnostic Criteria

In the DSM-5 the diagnostic criteria are as follows:
Repeated regurgitation of food over a period of at least one month. Regurgitated food may be re-chewed, re-swallowed, or spit out.

A. The repeated regurgitation is not attributable to an associated gastrointestinal or other medical condition (e.g., gastroesophageal reflux, pyloric stenosis).

B. The eating disturbance does not occur exclusively during the course of anorexia nervosa, bulimia nervosa, binge-eating disorder, or avoidant/restrictive food intake disorder.

C. If the symptoms occur in the context of another mental disorder (e.g., intellectual disability, or another neurodevelopmental disorder), they are sufficiently severe to warrant additional clinical attention.

Treatment

Untreated, rumination syndrome can damage the esophagus and cause unhealthy weight loss. If frequent rumination is damaging the esophagus, proton pump inhibitors may be prescribed. These medications can protect the lining of the esophagus until behavior therapy reduces the frequency and severity of regurgitation.

Health care providers typically treat the underlying condition with habit reversal behavior therapy. Individuals learn to recognize when rumination occurs, and to breathe in and out with the abdominal muscles (diaphragmatic breathing) during those times. Diaphragmatic breathing prevents abdominal contractions and regurgitation.

For people who have mental or developmental disabilities, treatment may escalate to mild aversive training–associating rumination with negative consequences–or other behavioral techniques.

Some people with rumination syndrome may benefit from treatment with medication that helps relax the stomach in the period after eating.

Other Eating Disorders (OSFED and UFED)

Linda, age thirty-five, is the mother of two children, ages one and three. She has been married for ten years to her husband and she works as a nurse practitioner. Linda's presenting problem is a concern about her weight. Linda reported she often feels ashamed and "like a hypocrite" when working with her patients, advising them to be healthier and make healthier choices when she is "clearly overweight."

Linda described she has never been a thin person, but has noticed her weight consistently rising in the past several years, especially in the most recent year after the birth of her youngest son. When describing her diet, Linda admitted she eats out for fast food daily. She attributed this to having "no time" to prepare adequate meals at home between her work and taking care of her children. In addition, she also described she experiences episodes in which she feels she has "no control" over what and how much she eats, relating there are many days she arrives home and eats an entire box of cookies or large bag of chips before she eats dinner.

Linda also shared she "hates her body" and the way she looks. She described she has not worn any type of form fitting clothing in years and is most comfortable in baggy shirts and hooded sweatshirts. She indicated she thinks about her looks every day and avoids looking in mirrors. Linda reported she does not understand why her husband is still with her or how he could even be attracted to her anymore. Linda stated food is controlling her life and she wants to lose weight and stop worrying about it so much.

Counseling interventions included working with Linda on identifying destructive thought patterns and distortional thinking. The counselor issued a Food and Feelings log for Linda to track her meals and the thoughts and emotions she experiences before and after eating. The counselor also provided psychoeducation regarding binge eating and body image issues. Linda was instructed to watch helpful documentaries and videos regarding how the media and marketing advertisers sometimes send harmful messages, especially for women. Linda was also referred to seek help from a dietitian to normalize eating and set goals to improve her diet, specifically regarding meal planning and preparation.

The wide range of eating disorders in Linda's story includes numerous other eating disorders grouped in two diagnostic categories. They include:

- Other specified feeding and eating disorders (OSFED)
- Unspecified feeding and eating disorders (UFED)

An OSFED can be any of three things.

1. It can be sub-threshold eating disorders (for example, a bulimic who only purges, on average, once every two weeks rather than once per week as the diagnosis of bulimia requires).
2. They can be mixed-types. For example, a woman may have some features of an avoidant/restrictive food intake disorder (ARFID) and anorexia, but not enough symptoms of either to warrant those diagnoses.
3. An OSFED can be a clear, even florid, pattern of disturbed eating that nonetheless is not otherwise recognized in the DSM-5. A "food addict" or compulsive overeater would be a clear example of a pattern of disturbed eating, usually leading to morbid obesity, that is not otherwise recognized within the DSM-5, so it would be diagnosed as an OSFED, and described as compulsive overeating or a food addiction.

These types of eating disorders can be as serious as the classic types, and they can also co-occur with other mental health issues that can range from alcoholism, to cutting, to compulsive shopping or bipolar disorder, among others. These unclassified eating disorders over time can contribute to severe health issues, can overlap with other disorders and are often complicated to diagnose and to treat.

Orthorexia Nervosa

Orthorexia nervosa is not currently recognized as a clinical diagnosis in the DSM-5, but many people struggle with symptoms associated with this term, coined by Steven Bratman, M.D. in 1997 and which literally means "fixation on righteous eating." Orthorexia occurs when individuals become obsessed with health related eating practices. The effects of semi-starvation mimic obsessive-compulsive disorder (OCD), which, as is seen in anorexia nervosa, further complicate and worsen the condition. Also, similar to individuals with anorexia nervosa who desire to be thin, these individuals become obsessed with what is considered to be "healthy eating."

Fiercely held internal rules and convictions can result in extreme and dangerous restricting behaviors and elimination of certain foods. Every day is a chance to eat correctly, rise above others in dietary prowess, and self-punish if temptation wins (usually through stricter eating, fasts and exercise). Self-esteem becomes integral to the purity of the orthorexic's diet, and they often feel superior to others, especially in regard to food intake.

Diagnosis and Treatment

Many people with symptoms of orthorexia also suffer from co-occurring disorders or addictive behaviors that make it difficult to regain a healthy relationship with food. Given frequent disagreement over the definition and nature of orthorexia, it's critical to confirm whether a person suffers from orthorexia, anorexia nervosa, another eating disorder, or co-occurring disorders. This critical step requires input from specialists in psychiatry, eating disorders, nutrition and family systems.

Treatment of orthorexia nervosa is very similar to that for OCD, with an emphasis on behavioral exposure with response prevention (ERP) and cognitive behavioral strategies (CBT). Cognitive behavior therapy is especially useful for treating OCD. It teaches the individual alternative ways of thinking, behaving, and reacting to situations that help them feel less anxious or fearful without having obsessive thoughts or acting compulsively.

Dialectical behavioral therapy (DBT) is used extensively in treatment of anxiety disorders. DBT combines behavioral, cognitive, and meditative therapies to help the individual heal.

Doctors also may prescribe medication to help treat orthorexia, with the most commonly prescribed medications for orthorexia being anti-anxiety medications and antidepressants.

Neurofeedback is a form of biofeedback designed to help people alter their brain waves in ways that can have a positive effect on their behavior, mood, and thinking. Neurofeedback provides information about the type and intensity of brain waves being generated.

PART II

Causes, Symptoms, and Effects of Eating Disorders

CHAPTER 4

Risk Factors and Underlying Causes

When Kimberly was twelve years old, she lived much the way an average kid lives. Her mother and father loved her very much, she went to a good school–where she excelled in science–and on weekends she played in the community soccer league. She was a pretty good offensive player, and every once in a while she even scored a goal for her team. Her friends were a typical bunch of girls who enjoyed hanging out at each other's houses talking about pop music, movies, and which boys were the cutest, or at least were not too gross. There was even talk about dating, although Kimberly's parents were aghast at the idea. Let the kids mingle at the mall, they said, where we can keep a sharp eye on them.

Over the summer before eighth grade, Kimberly's world fell apart. Abruptly, with no warning to Kimberly, her parents split up. Her father moved out. Her mother told Kimberly that her dad had a girlfriend and they wouldn't be seeing much of him anymore.

Her mom's income was barely enough to pay the bills, and even with child support from her dad, their standard of living deteriorated dramatically. When Kimberly went back to school in the fall, her status had changed. She could no longer afford to buy the cool clothes her friends wore and her phone was not the latest model. She didn't want her friends coming over to her house, which was increasingly unkempt because her mom was just too exhausted to maintain it.

While she did her very best to put on a brave front, the pain in Kimberly's heart was very deep and very real. With her social interactions and family life no longer a source of security and fulfillment, Kimberly found herself seeking comfort in something that she could do for herself.

At every opportunity, she started eating. It made her feel good. By the holiday season she had gained a few pounds.

When her father saw her, he frowned and said, "I can see by your appearance that you and your mom have no shortage of food in the house. I think you'd better lay off the cake and ice cream. Look at you—you're turning into a butterball. How can you play soccer like that?"

These words were like a knife in Kimberly's heart. She felt like whatever she did was wrong. There was no pleasing any of them—not her family, not her friends. She kept eating, but secretly, and then to avoid putting on weight she'd go to the bathroom and vomit. As the months passed her teeth began to show damage from exposure to stomach acids. Eventually her mother took her to the doctor, where she was diagnosed with bulimia nervosa. Then she began a treatment program focused not on any particular medical issue—she was a basically healthy person—but on intensive family therapy.

Understanding Eating Disorders

Eating disorders are a real health issue and a real mental health disease. They affect both sexes, all ages, and all races and cultures. The seriousness of eating disorders requires educating people about them, understanding them, and recognizing that they are treatable. Often because there is a stigma associated with an eating disorder, or the individual doesn't perceive it as a problem, many people don't seek help.

Eating disorders are complex conditions that can arise from a variety of potential causes: physical, emotional, social and familial issues. Once started, they can create a self-perpetuating cycle of physical and emotional destruction. They can involve extreme compulsive and obsessive behaviors that surround food, yet they are often not specifically about food. Rather, they are more about underlying emotional issues that require treatment in the form of psychotherapy, psychopharmacology, or both.

A wide variety of risk factors can increase the odds that an individual will develop an eating disorder.

Risk factors that involve control can rise from childhood when a child is subjected to external controls over how he or she should feel and look. Without being given a chance to express inner feelings, a child can develop a sense of working to please others, trying to achieve social acceptance and needing to conform to social demands. In the family circle, children's behaviors are influenced by the way they perceive the world is molded and their personality is shaped. Though most Western children are not either forced to eat or face starvation, the inherent development of social behaviors are formed when they are young. It is important again to note that no matter how much a parent tries to raise a child to become a healthy adult, there are so many other factors that come into play, that parents are not the sole, or even a primary, determinant of their child's mental health.

Four Parts of Temperament

Research suggests that an eating disorder is not always about the food. Eating disorders are based in a need to control, to cope with stress, and having a feeling of extreme anxiety with normal life functioning. The personality of the individual, which is the way that he perceives and interacts with the world around him, is affected by biology and experience.

As researchers Cloninger, Svrakic, and Przbeck wrote in 1993, temperament is defined as a biologically based predisposition to experience certain emotional and behavioral responses. Personality builds on temperament. They named four parts to temperament:

1. Novelty seeking, which seeks reward.
2. Harm avoidance, the need to avoid punishment by inhibiting behavior.
3. Reward dependence, a continued behavior that is being rewarded.
4. Persistence, which is the continuation of behavior that is no longer awarded.

Anorexia nervosa has been associated with low novelty seeking or uncaring about rewards, high harm avoidance, and high persistence. Bulimia is associated with high novelty seeking or the need for the reward of food, and high harm avoidance through binging. This demonstrates a conflict between the need for reward and avoid punishment.

Risk Factors

Trying to predict who will develop an eating disorder is difficult. Knowledge and understanding are also factors that will increase over time and hopefully create an atmosphere that encourages those with eating disorders or symptoms to talk about it. Environment, genetics, family dynamics, and culture can all contribute to causing eating disorders, but still those are not specific in themselves. Many people come from environments that are unhealthy, families that do not function appropriately and with genes that might very well predispose a person to develop an eating disorder but don't. None of these things is a direct cause of an eating disorder.

Research has shown that certain situations and events increase the risk of developing an eating disorder. These risk factors may include:

Age

Although eating disorders can occur across a broad age range including childhood, the teenage years, and older adulthood, they are much more common during the teens and early twenties. With remarkable consistency, research has shown that anorexia nervosa and bulimia nervosa typically occur during adolescence and that onset thereafter is relatively uncommon. The exception is binge eating disorder (BED), which may begin well into adulthood.

Over 95% percent of eating disorders affect youth between the ages of twelve and twenty-five, although many reported beginning prior to age eleven. Bulimia is more common among Latinos and African Americans than non-Hispanic whites in the United States, though non-Hispanic whites tend to have higher numbers of anorexia. A ten-year study conducted by the National Eating Disorder Association found 86% of young adults with eating disorders began before age twenty.

One of the factors that occur in children and youth that make eating disorders difficult to diagnose is extreme growth at that age. Parents have difficulty knowing what an average weight or eating behaviors of their child should be when they are growing so quickly. Weight loss is also a sign of so many other illnesses that often a diagnosis of an eating disorder is simply overlooked. Often the weight loss occurs so slowly that it is not noticed.

Being female

While males can have eating disorders, teenage girls and young women are more likely than teenage boys and young men to have anorexia or bulimia. Males are affected in approximately 10% of anorexia cases and 25% of bulimia diagnosis, but make up 45% of those who binge.

Genetics

Certain genes may increase a person's susceptibility to developing an eating disorder. Eating disorders are significantly more likely to occur in people who have parents or siblings who've had an eating disorder. A genetic influence may not be simply due to the inheritance of any one gene but the result of a much more complicated interaction between many genes and possibly non-inherited genetic factors as well.

Research by Kelly Klump, a professor of psychology at Michigan State University, has suggested that the origin of eating disorders has biological roots, similar to how bipolar disorder and schizophrenia are thought to have biological causes. Specifically, Klump's work found that when girls enter puberty their chances of developing such a disease grow rapidly. Before puberty, environmental factors alone were found to contribute to the development of various eating disorders. As puberty progresses, the genetic risk is activated and increases in importance to accounting for more than half the risk for eating pathology.

Family Factors

Family conflict, parental indifference, or its opposite -overprotective parenting- can be eating disorder risk factors. Family studies done with individuals who have been diagnosed with eating disorders find more anxiety, depression, disordered eating and compulsive behaviors within these individuals. There are traumas that the brain is forced to deal with that can become part of the convergence of factors that pushes a person into the cycle of an eating disorder. Anything that can cause emotional distress, if bundled with other risk factors, can move a person into the search for something to help them cope. Those coping mechanisms may be very unhealthy. Eating disorders can be used as punishment of self, control of self, and as a method to cope with life.

The presence of substance abuse, psychological issues, or a history of depression in a family can increase an individual's risk for developing an eating disorder. Families that fail to embrace a positive body image or are overly concerned with physical appearance can also contribute to the development of eating disorders. Research suggests that women with a mother or sister who has or has had anorexia nervosa are twelve times more likely than others to develop it themselves. They are four times more likely to develop bulimia.

Personality Issues

Certain personality traits, including a high drive for perfectionism, may contribute to the development of eating disorders. Individuals who struggle for perfection are at greater risk for developing anorexia or bulimia. This is because they have unrealistic expectations of themselves and others. In spite of their achievements–good grades or playing sports on a team–they feel inadequate, defective, and worthless. In addition, they view the world as black and white, no shades of gray. Everything is a success or a failure, good or bad, fat or thin. If fat is bad and thin is good, then thinner is better, and thinnest is best–even if it means looking skeletal and being rushed to the hospital with a heart attack.

As Pamela Keel and Jean Forney wrote in the *International Journal of Eating*, personality factors such as negative emotionality and perfectionism contribute to the development of eating disorders, but they may do so indirectly by either increasing susceptibility to internalize the thin ideal or by influencing selection of peer environment. During adolescence in particular, peers represent self-selected environments that influence risk. Consequently, peer context may represent a key opportunity for intervention, as peer groups represent the nexus in which individual differences in psychological risk factors shape the social environment and social environment shapes psychological risk factors. Thus, peer-based interventions that challenge internalization of the thin ideal can protect against the development of eating pathology.

Brain Chemistry

Research suggests that serotonin may influence eating behaviors. Serotonin is a naturally occurring brain chemical that helps regulate mood, learning, and sleep, among other things.

As reported by the University of Maryland Medical Center, the body's hypothalamic-pituitary-adrenal axis (HPA) may be a factor in eating disorders. This complex system originates in the following regions in the brain:

Hypothalamus. The hypothalamus is a small structure that plays a role in controlling behaviors such as eating, sexual behavior, and sleeping, and regulates body temperature, hunger and thirst, and secretion of hormones.

Pituitary gland. The pituitary gland is involved in controlling thyroid functions, the adrenal glands, growth, and sexual maturation.

Amygdala. This small almond-shaped structure lies deep in the brain and is associated with regulation and control of major emotional activities including anxiety, depression, aggression, and affection.

The teenage brain is a brain at risk with little else to push it in a positive direction. Brain research has determined that neural pathways continue to build beyond age twenty, suggesting that the teen brain has not yet fully matured and can create difficulty in learning, assessment of various situations, and making effective choices. The "reward system" in the brain fully develops before the cognitive systems. Added into that situation are anxiety, family issues, trauma, and other stressful situations that can cause the risk factors to grow. Giving young adults knowledge, understanding, support, and healthy choices is essential. Being present to help children build resiliency, deal with stress in healthy ways and to support them in choices and difficulties, likely helps to combat the probability of developing and maintaining an eating disorder.

Mental Health Disorders

People with depression, anxiety disorder, or obsessive-compulsive disorder are more likely to have an eating disorder. They often lack a sense of identity, and may try to define themselves by manufacturing a socially approved and admired exterior. They are often legitimately angry–for example, if they've been sexually abused as a child–but because they seek approval and fear criticism, they do not know how to express their anger in healthy ways. They turn it against themselves by starving or stuffing.

It is important to recognize that prolonged starvation induces changes in cognition, behavior, and interpersonal characteristics. It can therefore be difficult to discern the psychological *causes* from the psychological *effects* of eating disorders.

Validation through Dieting

People who lose weight are often reinforced by positive comments from others and by their changing appearance. This may cause some people to take dieting too far, leading to an eating disorder.

On the other side of the scale, if the mother and father preach and nag about junk food and try to limit their child's access to treats, the child may desire and overeat these very items. A 2003 study in *The American Journal of Clinical Nutrition* indicated that when parents restrict eating, children are more likely to eat when they are not hungry. The more severe the restriction, the stronger the desire to eat prohibited foods. These behaviors may set the stage for a full blown eating disorder in the future.

Mood Disorders

Mood disorders, which can cause extreme disability, are becoming increasingly prevalent. These are connected to the lack of a natural ability for the brain to balance good feelings with bad. Mood disorders include, major depressive disorder, dysthymia, atypical depression, seasonal affective disorder, bipolar disorder, and postpartum depression. Research suggests that low serotonin levels in the brain influence depression and mood disorders, and even though there is no test that measures precisely how much serotonin is available to the brain, a blood test can give a measure of the amounts. When the body produces too much serotonin, a person may have a depressed appetite.

Stress

Whether it's heading off to college, moving, landing a new job, or a family or relationship issue, change can bring stress, which may increase the risk of an eating disorder. Disordered eating may arise as a result of a death, loss, or abandonment. Because of an inability to mourn and/or cope, the individual will attempt to numb their feelings through restriction, bingeing and purging, or bingeing.

Sexual Abuse

Abuse, sexual assault, and incest–whether in the present or in the past– can also trigger an eating disorder. A history of sexual abuse is more common in individuals who suffer from eating disorders, suggesting that this is an eating disorder risk factor. Victims may find that their eating disorders help to emotionally protect them, repress or block out the memories, or numb their feelings. They may use the behaviors to try to take control of their lives, including avoiding sexuality and its negative associations.

As with all risk factors, correlations do not necessarily indicate causes. Abuse is a nonspecific risk factor, which means it can lead to many kinds of psychiatric problems, sometimes including eating disorders but often also including anxiety and depression. It's possible that people who are biologically predisposed to eating disorders are likely to have the eating disorder triggered by something as highly emotional and stressful as sexual abuse or any other form of trauma.

While it's important to understand that the trauma and the subsequent eating disorder are separate issues, they often become linked in the sufferer's understanding of them. Some eating disordered individuals feel that their behaviors are a rational mechanism for helping them to cope with their trauma and stress. For this reason, many sufferers are reluctant to give up their eating disorders.

Transfer Addictions

Alcohol and drugs can block out painful feelings, just like food or food deprivation can. Food, alcohol and drugs can all be used to self-medicate.

Some alcoholics and drug addicts develop eating disorders after gaining sobriety from alcohol and drugs, and some anorexics and bulimics develop drug and alcohol addictions after recovering from their eating disorders. Sometimes called a *transfer addiction*, in these cases they substitute one disorder for another.

Some sources estimate that up to 50% of all bulimics also suffer from alcohol or drug addiction. Substance abuse problems are believed to be less common among people with anorexia, but they still occur. Compulsive eaters may also become addicted to alcohol or drugs. Addictions and eating disorders may occur simultaneously or one may follow the other.

Sports, Work, and Artistic Activities

Athletes, actors, dancers and models may be at higher risk of eating disorders. Female gymnasts, ice skaters, dancers, and swimmers have been found to have higher rates of eating disorders. In a study of Division 1 National Collegiate Athletics Association (NCAA) athletes, over one-third of female athletes reported attitudes and symptoms placing them at risk for anorexia nervosa.

Male athletes are also at increased risk, especially those in sports such as wrestling, bodybuilding, crew, running, cycling, climbing, and football. Coaches and parents may unwittingly contribute to eating disorders by encouraging young athletes to lose weight.

Prader-Willi Syndrome

Prader-Willi Syndrome (PWS) is a complex genetic condition that affects many parts of the body. In infancy, this condition is characterized by weak muscle tone (hypotonia), poor growth, feeding difficulties, and delayed development. Beginning in childhood, affected individuals develop an insatiable appetite, which leads to chronic overeating (hyperphagia) and obesity. Some people with Prader-Willi syndrome, particularly those with obesity, also develop type 2 diabetes mellitus (the most common form of diabetes).

PWS can occur in any family, and cannot be prevented. There is no known cause. The condition affects only one in 12,000-15,000 people. Although considered a rare disorder, PWS is one of the most common conditions seen in genetic clinics and is the most common genetic cause of obesity that has been identified to date. Research continues to search for genetic markers to identify individuals who are prone to eating disorders.

Disrupted Brain Processing

The current research is based in brain imaging and the chemical make-up in the brain that exhibits abnormal or disrupted brain processing within eating disordered populations. If these factors can be regarded as the "causes" of the eating disorder, then the question cycles around to what is the cause of the disruption in the brain. Exposure to unhealthy environments, dysfunctional family life, poor eating habits, trauma, and mental illness can all contribute to the development of an eating disorder. All of these and more can create risks of chemical imbalances or disruption in the processes of the brain. Many individuals interviewed over time have admitted that they felt their own eating disorder began with extreme dieting, though not all felt this way. Often, as a person begins to control his or her diet and find success in losing weight, it initiates an abnormal fear that they can't stop and must constantly decrease food intake or increase exercise. The brain gets a good feeling about the weight loss and this "good feeling" is not something they are willing to relinquish. Instead, they want to extend it and increase it. What begins as a diet elides into an obsession.

CHAPTER 5

Sexual Orientation and Eating Disorders

Roger is a gay male who just graduated from college. During his high school years he had been in the closet, unwilling to reveal his sexual orientation to his mom and dad, who, he assumed, would have been bitterly upset and judgmental. He was also a member of the swim team, and the climate around the locker room was not always friendly concerning gay men. But at college, away from home and in a more relaxed environment, he had come out, and had even told his parents over summer vacation. They had survived the news–as he hoped they would–but Roger knew they were not happy. After he told them, their attitude was, "Okay, you told us you're gay. Let's not talk about it ever again. And please don't try to wear a dress or something, okay?"

Roger assured them that the last thing he ever wanted to wear was a dress.

He moved to the city, where he joined a gym. There he met a guy named Tony, who liked him but began to tease him about his weight. "Roger," Tony would say, "This is the big city. You've got to step up your game. You can't hang out at the gym and expect to meet the man of your dreams if you look like the Pillsbury Dough Boy. You need to get buff."

"But I like to eat," replied Roger.

"You need to eat healthy," said Tony. "No more junk food. No sugar. No white flour. Only organic. If you want a hot guy, you need to get six-pack abs. You need to get your body fat ratio down. Fat is bad. Okay?"

Lacking a personal compass–his parents weren't willing to give their son sensible advice–Roger dedicated himself to getting slim and fit. He became an expert in healthy eating, so much so that soon even his friends became annoyed at his zealous commitment. His eating choices became increasingly narrow and he began to look unhealthy. Eventually Tony took him aside and said, "Roger, I'm worried. You're taking this eating program too far. I think you may have orthorexia nervosa."

Roger told Tony to mind his own business. It was only after Roger was taken to the hospital for exhaustion and dehydration that he started to think about the road he was on.

Sexual Orientation

Eating disorders follow from a combination of complex factors. They may be behavioral, emotional, psychological, interpersonal and social, and usually are a combination of several of these factors. Risk factors in lesbian, gay, bisexual and transgender (LGBT)-identified individuals are unique to this population. Coming-out, harassment, bullying, and misunderstanding can push an LGBT individual toward coping with such oppression by the development of an eating disorder. LGBT populations are more likely to be homeless, discriminated against, have difficulty finding support and treatment, and lack family and cultural support within their circles.

The research on eating disorders is just beginning to extend itself to the LGBT stage. Studies are showing signs of eating disorders within the gay community, but also find that strong connections with gay community groups have a protective impact that is effective against the development of eating disorders. The feeling of acceptance and support has been found to counteract gender identity distress.

It is interesting to note that transgender individuals going from male-to-female can bring the same social conflicts with body image that occurs in non-transgendered women. A male who is now a female, or living as female, finds that society's standards regarding female beauty become a burden that constitutes a risk factor in her new existence as a woman. The need to appear physically beautiful is not unlike that of any other woman. So not only does the transgendered individual who goes from living as a man to living as a woman come with all the stress that any identity disordered person experiences, it also comes with the stresses that are put upon all women.

Diane Israel, describing her own experience as a transgender person, uses the word "confused." She describes life growing up as consistently confusing. This is not an uncommon developmental experience but it is compounded when the struggles related to gender identity are introduced into the mix. Her work as a psychotherapist has helped others through the challenges of coming out, developing socially supportive connections and also with resolving work-related problems. She helps those with gender identity issues that result in increased feelings of anxiety, depression, and low self-worth.

Learning to cope with such trauma often produces symptoms such as eating disorders. People who struggle with gender identity find it is just one more risk factor to add to the mix of other risk factors in their lives. One of the biggest factors that set up the transgender individual for increased stress is the loss of so many supports in life. Family, friends, work peers, employers, and our society in general, all contribute to the discomfort and confusion associated with the acknowledgement of a gender change in someone they know. Israel works on the basis that a person's well-being should not be tied to gender any more than it is to body image. What is not normal is the societal and cultural projections forced upon each person.

Gay Male Culture

Research shows that within the gay culture the male body is sexually objectified in much the same way as women's bodies are in the straight culture. This sexual objectification leads to obsessive body checking and comparing, and a desire to make the grade and be approved as sexually desirable.

Not measuring up to the gay ideal can lead to the development of body shame, which can lead one right into eating disorder behaviors in an attempt to deal with these stressful feelings and fears of being rejected by one's peers.

To stave off these feelings of shame about one's body, some gay men turn to extreme dieting. But restricting food intake, which itself is harmful, can also be a prelude for a binge where massive amounts of calories are rapidly consumed in an attempt to make up for the protracted calorie loss.

But a trip to the restroom to vomit, or several hours at the gym and a promise to oneself to keep dieting will take care of those feelings, or so one thinks. And thus the bulimic cycle is born. This cycle can produce guilt and even more shame, and an intense fear of becoming "fat" and a failed human being.

It is a cycle of secrecy and shame that can take on a destructive life of its own as the bulimia progresses and provides a false sense of comfort. For too many gay men this battle over their bodies starts at a very early age. Research shows one-third of gay men have a history of childhood sexual abuse, and that a history of childhood sexual abuse is often related to bulimia.

Although restrictive disordered eating is common in single gay men, it turns out that bulimic symptoms are actually more frequent in gay men who are in a relationship. It is postulated that these bulimic symptoms arise not so much because of a pressure to be thin as because of psycho-social difficulties within relationships.

Younger gay men (and lesbians who identify as feminine) are more susceptible to these socio-cultural pressures than older gay men, which may be due to less exposure to the media or to the fact that older gay men are more likely to be in a stable relationship. Being in a relationship has been shown to be a protective factor against restrictive disordered eating in gay men. In addition, some researchers have suggested that participation in the gay community, such as attending gay-affirmative events like Pride Walks, provides support that may help insulate gay men from developing eating disorders.

Lesbian Women

The story is somewhat different with lesbian women, who generally rate their appearance in one of three categories: feminine, androgynous, or masculine. Lesbians who consider themselves to be feminine have a similar risk of developing an eating disorder to their heterosexual peers; however, with androgynous or masculine lesbians, studies show their gender identity to be protective against eating disorders.

Research suggests that lesbians have relatively high levels of self-esteem regarding their bodies and sexual attractiveness. In particular, androgynous and masculine-identifying lesbians are more inclined to view themselves as being detached from societal and media-represented norms. They also have a decreased tendency to internalize cultural standards for physical appearance.

Lesbian women who have mostly lesbian and bisexual friends have a higher level of body satisfaction than lesbians who have mostly heterosexual friends. This may be because the latter group are more influenced by the straight culture's perceptions of what the female body should look like. Although most lesbians are no more likely to develop eating disorders than their heterosexual counterparts, and that some are protected from restrictive disordered eating such as anorexia, it has been shown that in both men and women, any same-sex sexual experience, no matter how infrequent, is predictive of an expression of bulimia. Again, this is thought to be a product of psychosocial functioning rather than societal pressures to be thin.

Transsexuals

The few existing studies of transsexual persons with eating disorders suggest that this group has an especially high risk of developing anorexia or bulimia. This is because both biologic males and biologic females who are transgender express significant body dissatisfaction. Many biologically male transsexuals equate femininity with slimness and aspire to be "ultra-feminine," highlighting their female characteristics. In contrast, biologically female transsexuals perceive that low body weight suppresses menstruation and secondary sexual characteristics. It is therefore not an attempt to attain thinness, which is not held to be a particularly masculine trait, but a desire to lose unwanted feminine characteristics which spurs dietary restriction.

In general, both biologic males and biologic females who are transsexual aspire to thinness in order to suppress their biological gender and accentuate the aspects of their desired gender. Gender reassignment has therefore been proposed as an appropriate treatment to alleviate the symptoms of eating disorders in transsexuals.

Dysmorphia and Dysphoria

When discussing those with gender dysphoria and body image disorder there can be some confusion in this area. It concerns the terminologies "dysmorphia" and "dysphoria."

Dysmorphia is when a person's body image does not align with reality. A person with anorexia nervosa might look at themselves in the mirror and say, "I'm fat," when in fact they are severely malnourished. They literally believe they're overweight.

Dysphoria is a sense of anxiety or distress about a person's body. It's when a transgender person says, "I identify as a woman, but I have the body of a man, and therefore I need to change my body to conform to how I see myself."

In other words, the feelings about one's body image being unrealistic, like a blindness to reality, is different from one who is just not happy in their body. Dysmorphia (false perceptions or a distorted body image) is seen as a mental illness where dysphoria (being unhappy about one's body) is not. However, a dysphoric individual can become dysmorphic and develop eating disorders, which are classified as a mental illness.

Dysmorphia, or seeing one's body as malformed when it is not, creates coping mechanisms in individuals to combat what, in their mind, is a truly malformed body—most often, too fat. The person with gender dysphoria does not have as a symptom an unrealistic image of his or her body, but rather an uncomfortable feeling with their gender.

Both can be treated, though in very different ways, to reduce stress, but that is where the similarity ends. That is not to say that a person with gender dysphoria cannot develop dysmorphia as well, because studies have shown that they do. But the differences need to be recognized. Therapy and medication used with the eating disordered person can help the condition, but therapy and medication offers little relief to the gender dysphoria patient unless that therapy and medication (and possibly surgery) are used in support of facilitating their transgenderism. In cases where plastic surgery is used to change the body of a dysmorphic individual, it may not offer relief from distress over body image. Transgendered individuals can be helped, if others support them in their transgenderism, where a dysmorphic person must be encouraged to think more realistically and to become more accurate and accepting of their bodies.

LGBT Research Studies

Compared to other populations, gay men are disproportionately found to have body image disturbances and eating disorder behavior. Gay men are thought to only represent 5% or less of the total male population but among men who have eating disorders, 42% identify as gay.

Compared with heterosexual men, gay and bisexual men have a significantly higher prevalence of lifetime full syndrome bulimia, subclinical bulimia, and any subclinical eating disorder.

However, current research suggests there are no significant differences between heterosexual women and lesbians and bisexual women in the prevalence of any of the eating disorders.

Between 2008 and 2011, a self-report questionnaire was distributed for the purpose of comparing heterosexual women with a history of eating disorders and individuals whose sexual identity was not heterosexual. It asked about mental health, substance use, sexual behavior, diagnosis of an eating disorder and nutrition history.

If the respondent reported an eating disorder, diagnosed or not, they were asked about the behaviors associated with that disorder. Specifically, they were asked about vomiting, use of laxative and diet pills during the previous month. From these reports it was found that 1.5% had been diagnosed with an eating disorder, 3% had vomited or used laxatives and more than 3% had used diet pills.

These results were mainly found in transgender individuals. Women who were unsure of their gender orientation and men who reported to be gay or bisexual were more likely to report a diagnosis of an eating disorder. In comparison to the control group of heterosexual women, female transgender students were four times more likely to report eating disorder diagnosis, use of pills and laxatives.

Transgender Individuals

Monica Algars from Abo Akademi University in Turku, Finland, examined a study by Edmonds, et al. Her examination of these studies concluded that transgender individuals often attempt to suppress their natural gender by becoming thin. In addition to the stress of living as a transgender person, they have the additional stress of trying to hide a body that makes them uncomfortable. This dieting can lead to eating disorders.

Algars stated that an increase in reported eating disorder diagnoses among transgender individuals might be caused by the population's increased involvement with mental health professionals over the last few years. She did find that gender reassignment treatment can help to resolve the eating disorders within this group.

Gender reassignment therapy is supported by cross-sex hormone therapy. Hormone therapy can balance the gender identity with the body's endocrine system through the use of testosterone-blocking agents, estrogen and progesterone. These can change the growth of breasts, soften skin, reduce or increase body hair, reduce erections, redistribute fat, change upper body strength and deepen the voice.

In studies that have shown an increase in eating disorders in men, they have also shown the increase mostly among gay or bisexual men. One study conducted by Feldman and Meyer targeted gay, lesbian, or bisexual men, and women recruited from New York coffee shops, bookstores and social groups. The presence of lifetime and current eating disorders was assessed using the DSM-5 categories of eating disorders. Though no statistical significance was reported between lesbian women and heterosexual women, there was a much higher incidence of bulimia among gay and bisexual men than among heterosexual men. There was a correlation that suggested that eating disorders in gender identity disordered men (now known as gender dysphoria) were found less when such men had more social interactions with other gay and bisexual men. This is an example that shows how having a support group around to help deal with stress can register a positive effect. This same study showed younger men ages twenty-five to thirty were more likely to have sub-clinical bulimia as opposed to full-blown bulimia. In sub-clinical bulimia the individual exhibits some, but not all, of the symptoms.

Prevalence Among LGB Men and Women

In their paper entitled "Eating Disorders in Diverse Lesbian, Gay, and Bisexual Populations," Matthew B. Feldman and Ilan H. Meyer surveyed 126 white heterosexuals and 388 white, black, Latino LGBT men and women. DSM-IV diagnoses of anorexia, bulimia, and binge eating disorder were assessed using the World Health Organization's Composite International Diagnostic Interview. The objective was to estimate the prevalence of eating disorders in lesbian, gay, and bisexual men and women, and examine the association between participation in the gay community and eating disorder prevalence in gay and bisexual men.

They found that gay and bisexual men had significantly higher prevalence estimates of eating disorders than heterosexual men. In both community and clinical samples of men with eating disorders, from 14% to 42%—compared with about 3% of the U.S. male population—are gay or bisexual. Consistent with these findings, studies have found that compared with heterosexual men, gay and bisexual men have more behavioral symptoms indicative of eating disorders. In contrast, there were no differences in eating disorder prevalence between lesbian and bisexual women and heterosexual women. They also found none across gender or racial groups.

Attending a gay recreational group was significantly related to eating disorder prevalence in gay and bisexual men. That is to say, the authors hypothesized that among gay and bisexual men, participation in body or appearance focused organizations in the gay community is associated with increased risk for eating disorders. Therefore, men who participate in organizations that emphasize physical appearance, such as a gay gym or sports team, will have a higher prevalence of eating disorders than men who are not affiliated with such organizations in the gay community.

The Bandini Study of People with Gender Dysphoria

A study done by Bandini, et al., compared persons with gender identity disorder (GID) (now called gender dysphoria) and those with an eating disorder, as well as with a control group. The groups included transgender individuals with genital reassignment surgery completed, those without genital reassignment surgery performed, others who had an eating disorder, those not diagnosed, and then compared them all to a large group of healthy individuals. The Structured Clinical Interview for Diagnostic and Statistical Manual of Mental Disorder, 4th edition, the Symptom Checklist (SCL-90) and the Body Uneasiness Test (BUT) were the primary tools in this assessment.

The control group of healthy individuals showed a lower psychiatric comorbidity and general severity than did those with an eating disorder. Those without genital reassignment surgery showed the highest levels on the Body Uneasiness Test as compared with those who had completed the sex reassignment surgery. Those with the surgery scored higher values than the control group on the Body Uneasiness Test. Their results showed that those with gender identity disorders developed a core of distress based in body uneasiness as a result of their gender identity crisis.

They found only a small connection to any general mental illness in gender identity disordered individuals who suffered from eating disorders. This raises the serious consideration that the stress of the gender disorder, and not some underlying pathology, may be the cause of the disordered eating in this population, unlike the broader general population.

CHAPTER 6

Dancers, Athletes, and Making Weight

When Julia was ten years old her mother enrolled her in ballet class. "She's so tall and slender," said her mom, "I just know she'll be a wonderful ballerina. She was born for it."

It was true–Julia was very good at ballet, and she worked hard at it. By the time she was in high school, she had appeared in the city ballet company's holiday production of The Nutcracker. Her mother was proud and Julia was on her way to a professional career.

Her biggest problem–at least to her ballet instructors–was that she enjoyed eating.

"You must have the correct lines," they would tell her and the other girls. Long legs, long necks, slender arms–the ideal was very clear. Womanly curves were not wanted.

"Ballet is a business," her mother would say. "You need to do what you have to do. No more desserts. No more cheeseburgers. No more potato chips. All of that food is your enemy. Eat healthy and take vitamins."

Many of Julia's fellow "bunheads"–as they were called because they all wore their hair pulled up in a tight bun–went further than just avoiding dessert. Many of them lived on a diet of coffee and cigarettes. Julia hated how she felt, not only because the restrictive diet was torture but because she often felt lightheaded. Her bones were fragile, too–another occupational risk of ballerinas who don't eat enough.

When she didn't get hired for the city ballet company, Julia made a choice to leave the business. The rigorous lifestyle and self-imposed deprivation just wasn't worth it any more. She went out and for the first time in years had a chocolate cupcake with sprinkles. She enjoyed every delicious bite.

Eating and Athletics

Dance–particularly ballet–is a highly competitive and physically demanding profession. In classical ballet, there is popularly believed to be an ideal "Balanchine" body type for women, with a preference for tall, slender women with long necks, long legs, and short torsos. Among dancers, eating disorders range from anorexia nervosa and bulimia to "disordered eating," a term coined by the women's task force of the American College of Sports Medicine for any chronic restrictive and ritualistic compulsive eating problems. The ongoing problem of eating disorders has created a minor industry of nutritionists and therapists specializing in dancers' emotional and physical problems.

Despite increasingly sophisticated methods, however, eating disorders in ballet remain extremely difficult to treat. When a ballet dancer is identified as having an eating disorder, she will require the same multi-disciplinary team involvement that anyone with anorexia or bulimia needs, but the cooperation of the dance school or company is essential as well. If she is underweight, dancing may have to be stopped or at least curtailed in combination with nutritional therapy to allow weight restoration to occur. This is likely to cause significant psychological stress, especially for a dancer who hopes to have a career in ballet, and supportive therapy must be provided–especially if the therapy if successful and the dancer gains weight, which may increase career anxiety.

Athletics

Participation in sports has many positive effects on athletes. They generally tend to live healthier lives than non-athletes, and they gain skills in teamwork, discipline, and decision-making that their non-athlete peers may not.

However, some aspects of the sports environment can increase the risk of eating disorders. That means athletes, and those who oversee athletics, must be vigilant to detect signs of trouble.

Athletic competition can be a factor contributing to severe psychological and physical stress. When the pressures of athletic competition are added to the cultural emphasis on thinness as well as any pre-existing risk factors for eating disorders, the chances increase for an athlete to develop disordered eating.

One area in which research findings are more definitive is for "lean" sports for which a thin or lean body, or low weight, is believed to provide a biomechanical advantage in performance or in the judging of performance.

Such sport body stereotypes can effect coaches' perceptions of athletes, and athletes who fit the desirably thin template are less likely to be identified as having an eating problem. Identification by coaches is sometimes influenced by sport performance; athletes are less likely to be identified if their performance is good.

The relationship between body image and body dissatisfaction in female athletes is more complex than in the general population. Sportswomen have two body images—one within sport and one outside of sport. An eating disorder can occur in either context or both. Additionally, some female athletes are conflicted about having a muscular body that is appropriate for sport performance but may not conform to the socially desired body type and may be perceived as being too muscular when compared to societal norms regarding femininity.

In a study of Division 1 NCAA athletes, over one-third of female athletes reported attitudes and symptoms placing them at risk for anorexia nervosa. Three risk factors are thought to particularly contribute to a female athlete's vulnerability to developing an eating disorder: social influences emphasizing thinness, performance anxiety, and negative self-appraisal of athletic achievement.

Male Athletes

Though most athletes with eating disorders are female, male athletes are also at risk—especially those competing in sports that tend to place an emphasis on the athlete's diet, appearance, size, and weight requirements, such as wrestling, bodybuilding, crew, and running.

Many more women suffer from the condition than do men; and so for men, this presents some problems, one being that most treatment programs are designed with women in mind. Other issues include more fear of being found out among men, and often a greater reluctance to seek treatment. The fact that eating disorders in men is often connected to seemingly legitimate weight control in sports gives the disorder some credibility as opposed to seeing it as unhealthy because, at least initially, it is done for instrumental reasons to enable or enhance performance. Men also sometimes will exhibit eating disorders in their pursuit of muscularity, which is more rarely seen in women, making it more difficult to expose.

While in the past few decades this has been changing, traditionally more boys have been involved in organized sports, where weight control increases success. Wrestling is especially concentrated around weight control, not allowing participation without strict weight limits. Track and field events, including running, require less weight to succeed and gymnastics is based on aesthetics. Swimming, bodybuilding, dance, and figure skating also have more body image associations than sports like football or basketball, where the body is less visible or is padded and covered more completely.

Other than association with a number of specific sports, eating disorders are less common in men who are athletic. There is a possibility that the eating disorders associated with these sports do not qualify to actually be called eating disorders since many of the typical "eating disordered" behaviors appear only during the sporting seasons.

Muscle Dysmorphia

Muscle dysmorphia is a predominantly male disorder. Sometimes called reverse anorexia, or "bigorexia" in the lay literature, muscle dysmorphia involves a distorted body image. But instead of seeing themselves as too fat, these men see themselves as weaklings, regardless of the amounts of exercise they pursue. They continually increase their workout routines and use whatever they can to increase lean muscle mass with high protein and anabolic steroids. Their goal is to bulk up and become buff in order to feel more powerful and have more presence. Because this behavior is cyclical, involves distorted body image, and involves excessive manipulation of their body with diet and drugs, it is considered by some as an eating disorder, but has yet to receive its own official classification within the American Psychiatric Association's DSM-5. Instead, muscle dysmorphia currently is diagnosed as a feeding and eating disorder- other specified, and the specification would be "muscle dysmorphia."

Body Dysmorphic Disorder

Many overweight men want to be smaller and may diet, but they do not harbor a distorted body image. More often, eating disorders begin in adolescence when boys hit puberty and have such growth spurts that they become thin until their bodies catch up with their growth in height. During this time, they can become obsessed with their body image and are more likely to use anabolic steroids in an effort to "bulk up", at a rate of somewhere between 4% and 12%. Anabolic steroids can adversely affect the liver, heart, and reproductive function. This body image distortion is a type of body dysmorphic disorder, which is classified under the category of Obsessive-Compulsive and Other Related Disorders, rather than as an eating disorder, per se.

Causes of Body Dissatisfaction Among Athletes

According to the *Eating Disorders Sourcebook* (3rd Ed; Judd) edited by Judd, there are three distinct factors that contribute to increased body dissatisfaction:

1. Social influences.
2. Performance anxiety.
3. Self-appraisal.

Each of these can affect how an athlete sees himself. This is particularly true in adolescence when the need to belong and be accepted can be so strong that teens will do almost anything to fit in. Some athletes have been in training all their lives and their parents and coaches, either intentionally or unintentionally, put so much pressure on these young men to be the best, that they can begin to translate failure into disappointment, feeling bad about letting their parents and coaches down. When this happens they may seek ways to make themselves feel better and the cycle of unhealthy choices begins. Other times the athlete puts so much pressure on himself that he seeks improvement and success to the point of doing whatever it takes to achieve that success, including engaging in unhealthy eating behaviors.

Athletes and Disordered Eating

If disordered eating patterns in an athlete is combined with other risk factors, the cycle of eating disorders can become part of that athlete's life. Symptoms for anorexia in athletes are the same as for the general population, and include significant weight loss, hyperactivity, depression, moodiness, distorted body image, fine, downy hair growth all over the body, feeling cold, excessive exercise, restricted food intake and obsessive-compulsive disorder. Symptoms for bulimia include the consumption of large amounts of food in a specific time period, binges followed by vomiting (or other types of compensatory behavior), eating in secrete, use of laxatives diet pills, excessive exercise, swollen salivary glands, dental problems and feeling of shame or depression.

Adults need to know the signs of disordered eating and not live in denial. Coaches and parents have to be involved in what their youth are doing, and signs of unhealthy behavior should be openly discussed and dealt with. These individuals who develop such behaviors need to be supported rather than shamed, and given understanding and help. It is easier to regain health if intervention occurs before the disordered eating escalates to the point of medical consequences or crisis.

Dieting Supplements Increase Risk

One of the major facilitators in male eating disorders is legal over-the-counter supplements. A study conducted by Richard Achiro, Ph.D., of the California School of Professional Psychology at Alliant International University, examined men 18 to 65 who visited a gym twice a week and used legal appearance- or performance-enhancing supplements that included whey protein, creatine and L-carnitine. Each participant was questioned in the areas of self-esteem, body image, eating habits and gender roles. According to Dr. Achiro, men no longer seek the bulk of Sylvester Stallone. The lean muscular look is in. In this study it was found that 22% increased their use of supplements over time even to the point of meal replacement. It was reported that 8% were told by their doctors to discontinue their use of such products and 3% had been hospitalized for kidney or liver problems caused by excessive use of these supplements. They concluded that men who used dietary supplements were at more risk for development of eating disorders.

Dr. Achiro noted that there should be more concern for these legal supplements and that the same attention should be given to them as is given to hormones and steroids or a variety of other illegal supplements. Men who abuse these products generally have significant dissatisfaction with their body image or an unrealistic view of their body (body dysmorphia). It was no surprise that the study by Dr. Achiro found a strong correlation between gender role conflict and legal supplement use, suggesting the role of insecurity about their masculinity as a factor in their unhealthy supplement use.

Dr. Achiro explains that it goes deeper than body image, per se, and extends to self-esteem and self-worth. The muscle-building supplements are the opposite of dieting, but the psychological aspects are very similar. The more the individual focuses on his body the more obsessive he becomes. Young men who are active in competitive sports in high school and college are often encouraged by their coaches to use supplements. This can have negative consequences. This study revealed that of all the participants, 29% knew they had a problem and many were not aware of the negative consequences. Others have noted that men diagnosed with body image disorder also experienced depression, anxiety and alcoholism or drug addiction at higher levels than those without body image disorders.

Social Media and Male Body Image

It has been clearly shown that social media has a negative effect on women and a healthy body image, but a study by Slater and Tiggemann, examined this effect on males. They found that teen boys who got involved in watching soap operas on television exhibited increasing drives for thinness and decreased muscularity. Music videos had the opposite effect. This particular study elicited input from predominantly white 9th and 10th graders from two different co-ed schools in Australia. Using the Drive for Thinness subscale of the Eating Disorders Inventory and the Drive for Muscularity scale, it was found that boys who watched reality television programs and read men's magazines was a good predictor of a drive for thinness. This study was limited in that the groups studied were fairly homogeneous and males who already show some obsessiveness with thinness and more often read men's magazines.

Changes In Male Toy Action Figures

In a research study by Pope, et al. of male toy action figures from *Star Wars*, the changes in what would appeal to boys in the figures of Luke Skywalker and Han Solo from 1978 to 1998 can be clearly seen. The earlier figures are slim and very average in physical appearance. The later models have exaggerated muscles in the chest, shoulders and thighs. The image of these toys went from a normal body image to one that is extremely muscular in an unnatural way. It can be compared with similar excessive features in the Barbie doll.

Specific Cases

Nina Emkin, a writer for the on-line magazine *The Fix Addiction and Recovery Straight Up*, wrote about why eating disorders are increasing in the male population. In her research she spoke to a young man who has been in recovery from anorexia for over ten years. He expressed how initially losing weight felt good but the more he lost the more it became an uncontrollable obsession or addiction and not at all about feeling good. She found that 10% of those with eating disorders are men, though many were not diagnosed. Emkin interviewed another man who was a twenty-eight-year-old construction worker. He reported that at the age of nineteen, he felt overweight and went on a strict diet. As time went on he cut more and more food out of his diet until he became extremely ill with malnutrition and was diagnosed with anorexia. He acknowledged that he lived with teasing all his life for his flabby middle section. He had feelings of low self-worth and never felt accepted by any peer group. Growing up in a family of muscular brothers he felt pressured to fit in so began to diet. It was a way to cope with his feelings until diagnosed with anorexia. Another young man who lost a few pounds as an adolescent, got so much positive attention for it, he just kept losing until he weighed seventy-two pounds. He admitted taping full bottles of shampoo to his middle and wearing a large shirt to hide them when he was required to weigh in each week by a doctor his family took him to see. Anorexia was never discussed until much later in his life.

For heterosexual men, the condition is sufficiently rare that doctors often don't consider it until the patient becomes disabled by malnutrition and suffers from severe illness connected with their eating disorder. Most of these men described growing up and being affected by the media into thinking that thin was the only way to be happy.

These men also confess that the feeling of their obsession is something they fight on a daily basis. They compare it to alcoholism in that you never fully become healthy. You are always an addict even though you may be a recovered addict and relapse is one diet away. Often these men feel ashamed and will not discuss what was happening. It sometimes takes severe health problems before they will admit what they are doing. These men sometimes feel that having a disease like anorexia, which has been attributed to mostly women, is demeaning to their masculinity. Control over the body becomes a way to exercise control over one's emotions.

Most eating disorders begin with another underlying psychological condition. Trying to manage this condition in order to function in life, too often results in unhealthy decisions that only make it worse. Getting an appropriate diagnosis and treatment has expanded greatly for women, but for men, getting the same attention for both diagnosis and treatment is advancing at a relatively slow pace. Education of families and physicians, and recognition of the symptoms by coaches, teachers, parents and others who are around adolescent boys is likely to improve awareness, diagnosis and treatment. These changes are gradually occurring, with "Eating Awareness" programs now becoming common elements of high school and college life. In time, research on eating disorders with men will likely catch up to the attention that has long been given to women, and both the similarities and the differences between the genders will become clearer in relation to the range and prevalence of disordered eating among them.

Support and Resources for Men

There is need for greater attention to eating disorders among men, and for consideration of more inclusive definitions of eating disorder that incorporate features that are more commonly part of men's experience. There also is a need for greater research attention to target the underlying causes of muscle dysphoria and the obsessive pursuit among men to build a massive physique and to pursue unhealthy patterns of eating. One organization that is dedicated to this cause is the National Association for Males with Eating Disorders or N.A.M.E.D. It was established in 2006 and is the only organization in the United States dedicated exclusively to the support of men with eating disorders and body dysmorphic disorders. The intent of this organization and their web site is to fill the gap with information, resources and support for men with body image disorders and their families. They are supported by the Academy for Eating Disorders (AED) and the National Eating Disorder Association (NEDA). Their website offers links to books, articles, and resources that have current information about the disorder, personal stories and up-to-date research.

CHAPTER 7

The Effects of Pregnancy and Medical Complications

*W*hen Rashida found out she was pregnant, she was delighted. She was happy in the same way any other woman would be happy. She had always wanted to be a mother, and she had often watched with a sense of envy as other woman played with their babies or pushed them in strollers. Being a mother seemed to her to be one of the most wonderful things that could happen to you.

Rashida was also terrified.

This was because the thought of putting on weight was horrifying. She saw how pregnant women looked. In her mind, they looked like whales. Their big bellies were so heavy that they had to lean backwards when they walked, making them look like overweight ducks. And the weird things they ate! Pickles and ice cream? The very thought made Rashida gag.

"It's not going to happen to me," she said to herself. "I'm not going to blow up like a Macy's parade float. I'm going to keep myself slender, the way I want."

Unfortunately, Rashida was not just "slender." At five foot six inches tall, she weighed only one hundred and ten pounds. Her mother had taken her to the doctor, who had sternly told Rashida that she was anorexic and needed to get counseling. But Rashida had gone to the group therapy sessions only a few times before dropping out.

"They're trying to make me get fat," she told her mother. "They keep telling me I'm too skinny! If anything, I need to lose a few pounds."

As the weeks passed and Rashida began to show her pregnancy, her mother became consumed with one mission in life: to get her daughter to eat enough food to keep both herself and her baby healthy. It would prove to be a full-time job, and with every passing week her mother hoped that Rashida would eat just a little bit more. But Rashida was stubborn and resourceful, and her mother never knew a moment's rest.

Pregnancy and Eating Disorders

For a woman with an eating disorder, ordinary daily life can seem very challenging. The stress is compounded when the woman is also experiencing either pregnancy or a separate medical complication or condition.

Pregnancy and motherhood require a great deal of energy and strength. During pregnancy, the growing baby receives all its nourishment from the mother's body. The mother's body will prioritize its allocation of resources in favor of the fetus, and if the mother's nutritional reserves are not sufficiently restored through healthy eating, the mother can become severely malnourished. This can lead to depression, exhaustion, and many other serious health complications.

The average woman gains thirty pounds during pregnancy. For women with eating disorders, having to gain this amount can be very stressful. While some women with disordered eating more easily cope with weight gain during pregnancy because they see it as a sacrifice for an important cause, others may fall into deep depression as they struggle with the tension between the idea of weight gain and their body image issues.

Pregorexia

Pregorexia is a non-clinical term used to describe the presence of anorexia-like symptoms in pregnant women. Pregorexia has the same basic symptoms and risk factors as anorexia, the difference being that there is another life involved that depends upon the mother's nutritional and food intake. Women with the disorder have an excessive fear of pregnancy-related weight gain and use various methods, including extreme exercise routines and calorie restriction, to avoid the weight increases that mark the course of a normal, healthy pregnancy. Potential consequences of these behaviors include pregnancy complications, premature childbirth and a variety of health conditions associated with an unusually low child birthweight.

Conditions that complicate a pregnancy and are caused directly by an eating disorder include miscarriage, poor nutrition, dehydration, cardiac irregularities, premature births, labor complications, nursing difficulties and depressions. The restriction of food will affect the mother before it affects the baby. The baby's development is biologically primary. Experts have suggested that purging, restrictive food intake, and use of laxatives or diuretics, however can lead to harm to the baby during development that can be observed early or even during later years as the child grows. Risks to the baby include retardation, poor growth, low weight, low APGAR scores (for Appearance, Pulse, Grimace, Activity and Respiration), respiratory problems, difficulty eating, neurological defects if excessive exercise is involved, and Attention-Deficit Disorder. Any woman who has a history of eating disorders, demonstrates new feelings of body image issues during pregnancy, is ambivalent about the pregnancy, has relational issues, or surrounds herself with those who pressure her to stay thin, are more at risk than others. Societal pressures can be seen in the pregnancy of celebrities who gain little weight and look normal right after delivery.

Women who are pregnant do show signs of being at risk if they become preoccupied with weight gain, weighing themselves, excessive exercise, becomes over critical of her body shape, gains very little weight, does not appear as large as she should be at different stages, continues dieting or appears depressed. A woman with an active eating disorder who becomes pregnant should immediately end all eating disordered behaviors, talk to the obstetrician about the eating disorder, gain the appropriate recommended weight, and work with professionals in depth to make sure both mother and baby stay healthy.

When a pregnant woman limits her food intake, she limits the nutritional needs of her baby and herself. During 1944, in Holland, when the Germans occupied their area and starved the people, pregnant women especially suffered. Called the Dutch Hunger Winter, it went on for several months. There were long term studies done on children born during this time and much was learned about the effects on the children. Robert Sapolsky, a Stanford professor of neurology, made a documentary in 2011 about the effect such starvation has on the fetus. His film revealed that during the second and third trimesters, a fetus is developing neurologically according to the environment of the womb. These children developed a sense that the environment surrounding them was cruel. Their cells had to adjust to survive. Their bodies had to raise the capacity to store fat. Later in life these individuals developed more psychological disorders, cardiovascular disease, and metabolic syndrome than shown in others.

One conclusion is that stress suffered by the mother is passed on as stress to the fetus and the consequences of that stress reveals itself throughout their lifetime in various unhealthy ways. Statistical data that has been reported from various studies show that first-time pregnant women have a 25% to 44% chance of development of binging or bulimic behaviors. Like with other eating disorders, physicians, friends, and family must be observant and know the signs.

Kathryn Balch blogs for the ABC online website, and in 2011 wrote about pregnancy and eating disorders after interviewing many moms and their experiences. One of the problems Balch found was that pregnant women with diagnoses of eating disorders often keep it a secret from their obstetrician. Because pregnancy in itself offers a risk due to sensitivity about body image, a pregnant woman who has an eating disorder needs to think of herself as having a medical condition that must be monitored with her doctor. And because purging can be hidden as morning sickness, a person with a diagnosis of eating disordered has to know the complications that can arise.

Clariss Bonanno, an obstetrician who works at Columbia University and deals with high-risk pregnancies, admits that eating disorders in pregnant women are grossly under diagnosed. Because eating disorders are based in anxiety, pregnancy can increase that anxiety and coping behavior to control what feels to be out of control. A growing baby within a woman can have that feeling of dealing with a body out of control.

One mother Balch interviewed was a blogger who had never blogged about her eating disorder. But in the initial months of her pregnancy, she did, though she did not publish it. After a few months she began to struggle so much with the weight gain of the pregnancy she sent the blog to her family. They were shocked to find out that she was suffering so much without their knowledge and that they even unwittingly contributed to her illness by routinely complimenting her on her thinness. She was finally able to publish her blog and began to see her experience as one that might help others to share their own experiences with friends and family and elicit the support they needed throughout the pregnancy process.

Responses to Pregnancy by Expectant Mothers

Even for a woman who has been in recovery from an eating disorder for a long period of time, pregnancy can trigger old habits and behaviors with the new changes and symptoms typically experienced during this time.

In 1989, Dr. Raymond Lemberg Ph.D., and Jeanne Phillips described in *The International Journal of Eating Disorders* their study that examined the impact of pregnancy on anorexia nervosa and bulimia. A survey of women with an active eating disorder involving anorexia nervosa, bulimia, or mixed symptoms six months prior to their first pregnancy was undertaken to gain information on their attitudes toward becoming pregnant, their fears and concerns related to the unborn child, and the impact of the eating disorder behaviors both prenatal and postnatal. The survey included the mother's weight gain and weight gain of the baby as an indicator of its health, and the obstetrician's view of the pregnancy and health status of the infant upon delivery.

The results indicated that pregnancy had a pronounced *beneficial* impact on anorexic and bulimic symptoms during pregnancy. Many of the expectant mothers were both willing and able to control their eating disorders during their pregnancy. In contrast to previous research, infants had normal birth weights and deliveries with an absence of congenital defects.

However, researchers noted that lasting psychological benefit was limited to a minority of the sample in the first year after childbirth. Once the baby was born, many of the surveyed mothers reverted back to their pre-pregnancy condition.

Another study came to a different conclusion. In 1994, Linda Lewis and Daniel le Grange investigated the impact of pregnancy on six expectant mothers suffering from bulimia nervosa. The six women completed several rating scales and participated in a semi-structured interview. The information was used to construct a narrative of the subjects reflecting their eating habits during and following the pregnancy. During the course of pregnancy, the women expressed fears including losing control of their eating and weight, causing damage to the unborn child by engaging in bulimic practices, and not being able to cope with a newborn infant.

With regard to eating pathology during pregnancy, unlike the previously cited study, the six women did not experience amelioration in bulimic symptoms. In the puerperium (the period of about six weeks after childbirth during which the mother's reproductive organs return to their original nonpregnant condition), there was a resurgence of bulimic symptoms for all women either at a level of severity equal to or worse than before conception. While the sample size was small, in this case pregnancy did not seem to provide women with an opportunity for recovery from bulimia nervosa, and in some cases resulted in an exacerbation of bulimic symptoms.

The psychological effects of an eating disorder can have a tremendous impact on the mother's mental health, particularly if the disorder is left untreated. Some of the psychological effects that may be experienced by the mother include postpartum depression, anxiety or panic attacks, low self-esteem, poor body image, and even suicidal ideations.

Miscarriage

Because of dramatic advances in fertility technology, women with anorexia nervosa, even those who are at low body weight and amenorrheic, may be able to conceive. These women will also need intense prenatal care because they face a higher than normal risk of obstetric complications, particularly miscarriage.

Normal weight gain during pregnancy may intensify concerns about shape and weight in a woman with anorexia nervosa, and this may contribute to inadequate prenatal energy and nutrient intakes, leading to miscarriage, low birth weight or premature infants, and other birth complications.

Research suggests that women with a history of anorexia nervosa have nearly twice as many miscarriages as the average. However, the rate of miscarriage may not differ between women who are actively anorexic during pregnancy and those who have had anorexia nervosa in the past.

Women who are underweight before they conceive may be able to reduce their risk of miscarriage in the first trimester simply by taking prenatal vitamins that contain folate and iron, and by eating several servings of fresh fruits and vegetables each day.

In addition to an increased chance of having a miscarriage, having an eating disorder while pregnant can create other health risks for mother and baby. These can include premature labor or premature birth, stillbirth, respiratory problems for the baby, preeclampsia or pregnancy-induced hypertension, an increased risk of cesarean section, jaundice, placental separation, having a low-birthweight baby, complications with labor, delay of fetal growth, gestational diabetes, an increased risk of birth defects, and depression during pregnancy or post-partum depression.

Eating Disorder Treatment During Pregnancy

Eating disorders often go undetected by general practitioners; research suggests that only 10% of women with bulimia nervosa are identified and only half of these are referred for treatment. Prepregnancy counseling sessions and the first antenatal visit are good opportunities to screen for eating disorders, as women are perhaps more open to advice and help at these times. Guidelines published by the National Institute for Health and Clinical Excellence recommend opportunistic screening in vulnerable groups.

For women who struggle with an eating disorder, there may be intense feelings of guilt or shame during pregnancy. Perhaps the woman may feel dissociation with her growing baby, and engaging in anorexia, bulimia, or another disorder can further this disconnection.

In addition to the many changes that are rapidly occurring in a new mother's life, for an expectant mother with an eating disorder accepting the reality of the responsibilities as a parent can be difficult. Because of the physical, mental, and emotional connections with an eating disorder, it's not just something that can easily be stopped, even by a well-intentioned mother in pregnancy.

If a woman is suffering with an eating disorder and is currently pregnant, it is important she seek the help and treatment she needs to promote a healthy outcome for her and her baby. Effective eating disorder treatment during pregnancy should include regular visits with her obstetric doctor to closely track the growth and development of the baby; a counselor or therapist who can help guide her through any fears or concerns she may be facing; and a nutritionist, who can help ensure the mother is consuming adequate nutrition for her and the baby.

Finding a support group and attending pregnancy or parenting classes can also be helpful.

If necessary, higher levels of care may be required to help a woman who is pregnant and dealing with an eating disorder. This may be true in circumstances where a woman is severely dehydrated, has electrolyte imbalances, cardiovascular complications, or other psychiatric issues that may put her or her baby in danger. In these scenarios, the best form of treatment may be at an inpatient or residential level of care, in which healthcare professionals closely monitor the woman and her growing baby.

A Genetic Predisposition

Genetic studies identified chromosomes numbered one and ten can increase the chance of developing an eating disorder. If a child's mother or sister display eating disordered behaviors, the chance for the child have an eating disorder increases dramatically. Not only does the child have a risk factor genetic set, living in an environment with a person who has an eating disorder will model unhealthy attitudes and behaviors. For some women, becoming pregnant is overwhelming. First they lose their waistline, then they have to opt for larger clothes that aren't so flattering, and exercise is made more difficult; and later in the pregnancy, there is often sleep deprivation. All of these are very normal unless you suffer from a mental illness, and then the anxieties explode and coping with them only increases the need for more control. There is a real and great fear that letting go of their eating disorder, their severe limitations on eating or their purging will just be the hole in the dike that will eventually burst open and lead them to an unsightly body. And for this kind of mental illness, life surrounds the distorted image the woman has about her body. It is a struggle that must be fought moment to moment.

Self-Harming

Another complication that can disrupt with those who are eating disordered are self-injurious behaviors, or SIB. These are behaviors that cause harm to the body because it is a release for extreme emotional distress. It is usually seen in children between the ages of ten and fourteen, though it has been seen in children as young as seven, and is often accompanied with an eating disorder. Hurting oneself can appear as slicing, burning, punching, scratching, hair pulling or cutting. The severity ranges from superficial to needing medical care. Eating disorders are obsessive-compulsive behaviors in an effort to control life that feels out of control. It is the same with self-harming behaviors. It is a person's coping mechanisms to deal with stress, anxiety and depression. It can be a means of punishing themselves, making their inner feelings visible or for a release of endorphins to increase good feelings in the brain and it is addictive. The problem is the cutter has to continually increase the pain to get the high, which means they cut deeper and longer over time.

One of the side effects of eating disorders is the impact it has on a person's social life. Trying to hide the disorder, dealing with physical well-being, and just day to day functioning become difficult. Medically the body may deal with severe constipation, abnormally low heart rate, abdominal distress, dry skin, hypotension, cardiovascular problems and changes in brain structure. Osteoporosis and kidney dysfunction are also affected. A woman's body can experience amenorrhea or a loss of the menstrual cycle, cancer of the esophagus, disrupted blood sugar levels, liver problems and extreme fatigue syndrome. A weakened immune system may develop, diabetes, digestive difficulties, edema and electrolyte imbalances. Electrolyte imbalances will affect all organs, cells, joints, and circulation.

When a person reaches out for help with an eating disorder, the underlying mental illness must be addressed as well as the medical conditions that the body will have succumbed to during the time the eating disorder has been present. The entire affair is a complex mix of physical, psychological, and social issues that require professional help with a program that offers all of this, including nutritional counseling. A person who decides to seek help has taken the first step toward a healthy life and often that first step is the most difficult. Once the person has given themselves up to the help of others, they will automatically feel a relief of one layer of stress, though initially opening up to others creates some stress.

Any total change of lifestyle is definitely a hill to climb, a mountain to conquer and the creation of a different way of thinking. For a person who is physically depleted, socially numb and psychologically addicted, the change comes close too impossible. But it is not. Part of the treatment programs is showing the patient there is hope.

The Internet has helped individuals to open up and share their lives, struggles, and hope. It offers everyone an immediate support group, no matter what your gender, social class, economic level, race, culture or other differentiations. As many people as there are who have an eating disorder there are that many variations of the disease. What is important is to open up, reach out to others for help and support, and take the first step toward recovery.

PART III

The Way Forward—
Research and Treatment

CHAPTER 8

Psychodiagnosis and Research Methodologies For Eating Disorders

S *ylvie was forty-eight years old when, after twenty-five years of marriage and two children, she got divorced. While the separation was amicable, it was a blow to her self-esteem. She couldn't help but think that if she had been more attractive, her husband would have made more of an effort to stay married to her. And she imagined–without having any real evidence–that he would soon be dating a younger, more slender woman. After all, isn't that what all divorced men do? Even if they're out of shape and have an expanding waistline, for men it was somehow, and very unfairly, different. They were held to a different standard than their ex-spouses.*

Sylvie's problems began when she started thinking about dating again. She looked around her and saw–or at least she thought she saw–that all the other available women were slim and trim. Of course this wasn't really the case, but Sylvie saw it that way.

And as her adult daughter reminded her too often, if Sylvie wanted to swim in the dating pool, she needed to lose some weight and get herself in shape. This only added to her body image insecurity.

There's nothing wrong with wanting to be healthy and attractive, but Sylvie took it one big step further. She developed an eating disorder that revolved around food deprivation combined with a dependency on diet pills.

To compound the problem, her children were leaving home, which can prove highly traumatic for some mothers. This is especially true when a woman is defined by her children and her primary identity is that of being a mother. Without children to validate her role as mother, Sylvie began to feel worthless. Focusing on appearance, diets, health, and exercise filled that empty space and provide new identity.

In the aftermath of the divorce, Sylvie struggled with fears of spending the remainder of her life alone. Returning to the world of dating caused her extreme anxiety and insecurity. In order to achieve a younger, thinner, and more desirable body, she turned to extreme measures to lose weight.

The path towards the successful diagnosis and treatment of eating disorders has been long and roundabout. In the twentieth century, researchers leaned towards psychosexual developmental theories such as Freud's oral stage. For example, this focused on a description of anorexia as being due to a disruption in the parent-child relationship or more specifically the mother-child relationship, resulting in a personality disorder with fragmented thoughts, narcissistic self-absorption, splitting of the ego, and regressive mental functioning. This theory pointed to the resulting oral masochism of the anorectic. This theory, along with the related formulations of object relations theory, suggested that people have a basic inner drive to form relationships, and the failure to form successful early relationships creates difficulty later in life.

In 1973, Hilda Bruch examined this line of thought in her research and suggested that these relational ruptures were not a *cause* of anorexia nervosa but rather a *consequence* of it. Her ideas were that AN was a search for self-respective identity in the context of autonomy-inhibiting parents, including an arrested conceptual identity and a delusional disturbance in body image, which is merely a symptom of a much wider misperception of self and feelings of ineffectiveness.

Assessments

Over the next decade, object relational theories integrated with the identity delusion theories and further studies pointed towards eating disorders being more related to borderline personality disorders than to psychosexual developmental disruptions. This created the relationship to the intrapsychic structures, which further held to the notion that this illness was a disturbance within an individual, specifically a fragmented and helpless ego. This turn in thinking continued and offered a better basis for more valid and reliable testing. The idea that the disorder was more linked to what was going on within the personality of the individual as the cause of anorexia nervosa, instead of what took place between the mother and the child, led the way to begin assessing patients with measures already in common use.

Such testing has been based on two different types of tests. One is *projective tests* and the other is based in *objective tests*. Early work tended to utilize projective assessments, consistent with the more psychoanalytic and object-relational perspectives that dominated at that time, though objective testing has since become the more common approach to assessment.

Repairing Ego Functioning

By 1982, newer studies examined the objective side of the patient with an eating disorder. Over time these assessments have allowed for the comparison of the personality characteristics of anorectics with other forms of mentally illness. The AN individual typically expresses a disturbed sense of reality, impairment of ego functioning, ineffective ego defenses (or coping mechanisms), and poorly managed affect and thinking disturbances. Given these findings, treatment turned to focus on efforts to repair ego functioning.

Psychoanalytic therapies have not been particularly successful with eating disordered patients in part because this form of therapy relies on an individual's motivation and interpretation of events, which are often compromised features of individuals with eating disorders. This failure led researchers to aim their treatment at methods that do not rely on interpretation or the cultivation of insight as a mechanism for overcoming disordered eating.

Behavior modification was a natural treatment alternative in this regard. But, while weight gain can be successful with this method, it is not designed to address the restoration of any ego functioning or the cognitive or emotional elements of the disordered eating.

In 1984, Arnold C. Small discussed the psychodiagnosis of eating disorders, mainly anorexia nervosa, and research methodologies being used. At that time the main focus was on anorexia nervosa because it was more broadly recognized and more severe than other eating disorders.

Current neurobiological studies have connected many of the symptoms of eating disorders with the body's neurological workings, giving hope for the development of more effective interventions. This treatment is often referred to as *temperament-based treatment* and uses observation and experience with these disorders to develop individually tailored interventions. This creates interventions based on previous trials and experience that target the symptoms exhibited in the behaviors observed.

Such treatments involve increasing mindfulness and the use of cognitive therapy. It involves training the patients to disconnect from depressed thinking that may increase the behaviors. Thinking that involves negative body image or feelings of low self-worth can be a target for treatment by restructuring the person's thoughts. This therapy, combining mindfulness training with cognitive behavioral therapy, has been assessed through trials over a sixty-week period and found to significantly reduce the recurrence of episodes of the inappropriate eating-related behaviors.

Biological, Neurological, and Behavioral Factors

To develop treatment beneficial to the specific eating disorder expressed by an individual, treatment programs must target the underlying neurobiological mechanisms and develop an understanding of how these are manifested behaviorally through the individual's particular personality. When these three factors are determined, the treatment umbrella can integrate building in more constructive coping strategies that focus on all factors; biological, neurological, and behavioral.

Alexithymia and Eating Disorders

Alexithymia refers to the diminished capacity to experience or express emotions. It includes difficulty identifying different types of feelings, a limited understanding of what causes feelings, difficulty expressing feelings, difficulty recognizing facial cues in others, limited or rigid imagination, constricted style of thinking, hypersensitivity to physical sensations, and detached or tentative connection to others. First mentioned as a psychological condition in 1976, recent studies have found it has two dimensions.

1. A *cognitive dimension* where the individual struggles to identify, interpret and verbalize feelings or process emotions.
2. An *affective dimension* where there is a substantial retardation in reacting, expressing, feeling and imagining or experiencing feelings.

Individuals with eating disorders may have elevated levels of alexithymia, particularly difficulties identifying and describing their feelings. A number of theoretical models have suggested that individuals with eating disorders may find emotions unacceptable and/or frightening and may use their eating disorder symptoms, including restricting food intake, bingeing, and/or purging, as a way to avoid or cope with their feelings.

As Matilda E. Nowakowski, Traci McFarlane, and Stephanie Cassin wrote in 2013, when compared to healthy controls, the majority of studies focusing on eating disorders have found higher levels of alexithymia in individuals with eating disorders and disturbed eating. When the individual characteristics of alexithymia are examined, individuals with eating disorders have difficulty identifying and communicating their feelings.

It has been suggested that patients use maladaptive eating behaviors–bingeing, purging, dietary restriction–and excessive exercise as a way to avoid or cope with their emotions. Specifically, when a child experiences a home environment in which emotions are viewed as unacceptable or frightening, the child may develop the belief that emotions are bad and should not be experienced or expressed. Subsequently, each time that an emotion is experienced these beliefs become activated. This activation leads to a secondary emotion such as shame, guilt, or disgust that arises in response to experiencing an emotion. For example, if the child feels great happiness, the fact that a strong feeling is present triggers a response of guilt or shame. These secondary emotions increase the patient's distress and decrease his or her coping abilities, thus leading to engagement in eating disorder behaviors in an attempt to avoid or cope with the emotion.

Difficulty Tolerating Negative Internal States

In addition to the underlying features of alexithymia, those with anorexia also demonstrate great difficulty tolerating negative internal states and may have a diminished capacity to attend to body cues. For example, researchers have found that some anorectics are unable to even detect their own heartbeats. It is believed that this disturbed self-awareness of feelings contributed to their diminished response to hunger cues, the skewed body images, and lack of recognition to symptoms of malnutrition or motivation to change in the anorectic person. Specifically, distorted body image, lack of recognition of the symptoms of malnutrition, and diminished motivation to change, appeared interrelated in individuals with anorexia nervosa. Assessing the extent of disturbance in relation to these factors within anorectic individuals can help lead to the development of a more effective diagnosis and treatment plan.

Assessment Questionnaires

Over the past three decades there has been an increase in the research regarding the assessment and treatment of eating disorders. Questionnaires remain the assessment tool of choice and include self-reports, diagnostic questionnaires based on the DSM, screening questionnaires, measurements for quality of life, specific eating disorders, and for commonalities of eating disorders.

In 2001, Carlos M. Grilo of the Yale University School of Medicine compared various methods of assessment of eating disorders in relation to binge eating disorder (BED). With forty-seven patients already diagnosed, he used the Eating Disorder Examination Interview (EDE) and the Eating Disorder Examination Questionnaire (EDE-Q). Thirty-seven of these individuals participated in a four-week study to monitor their own eating behaviors and returned to complete another EDE-Q (questionnaire). The findings revealed no significant differences in the scores of the EDE and the EDE-Q over time in the area of binge eating and overeating episodes. However, the second assessment, EDE-Q, showed significantly higher scores in the category of overeating, on dietary restraint, eating concerns, weight concerns and body shape concerns but with a close correlation between the earlier and later scores. This suggests that the questionnaires were fairly reliable and that self-monitoring on a regular basis caused the patient to answer more realistically as to the number of occurrences in areas other than binge eating and overeating episodes.

Genetic Factors and Environmental Factors

In 2011, Laura M. Thornton and others assessed the genetic factors influencing eating disorders. The increase in these genetic studies have notably indicated that genes do contribute to individuals with anorexia nervosa, binge-eating disorder, bulimia nervosa, and purging disorder. The findings imply that prevention of these disorders could be increased with more attention to the genetic epidemiological research.

This study specifically implied that a focus on endophenotypes can increase the size of populations available for study and potentially yield a more genetically homogenous population.

Endophenotypes is a genetic branch of research used to identify stable phenotypes with genetic connections. Endophenotypes are measurable biologic markers for disease and help clarify which traits are more heritable and influence biological, neurocognitive or psychological processes.

This specific study provided strong evidence that genetic factors do contribute to the etiology of a variety of eating disorders. An "item factor" approach was applied in the examination of both genetic and environmental studies. This method allowed for the association between the specific eating disorder diagnosis and the symptoms using factor scores. The scores given the genetic, shared environmental and unique environmental factors of liability are then used to determine an overall diagnosis. This study connects the endophenotypes and the criteria relating to the diagnosis, which will facilitate future diagnosis based on endophenotypes. If a child is tested and the endophenotypes scores highly correlate with the connected factors in the study, then this child could be regarded as having a greater heritability for disordered eating.

Need for More Diversity in Research

Research on eating disorders has traditionally studied primarily Caucasian girls. More diverse samples and methods are needed to challenge the notion that eating disorders primarily occur in Caucasian girls in the United States. Likewise, the field has developed an over-reliance on cross-sectional, correlational studies. In order to test a wider range of hypotheses and develop a fuller understanding of disordered eating, researchers need to use a broader range of methods. These include longitudinal studies, experimental research studies, and naturalistic investigations.

Retrospective vs. Prospective Studies

Longitudinal studies are divided into two basic types, *retrospective follow-back* investigations and *prospective follow-up* investigations.

A retrospective follow-back investigation is used when the eating disorder in an individual is already known and the researcher is studying the kinds of factors that may have contributed to the development of the disorder. In this type of longitudinal study, the client is compared to another person with similar sex, age, and racial/cultural background but with no history of eating disorder. The history of each person or group, is compared environmentally in relation to a wide range of variables such as parental problems, disruptive events, parent psychiatric disorders, teasing and bullying, and sexual and physical abuse. Their personal vulnerability may also be compared, including childhood characteristics, premorbid psychiatric disorder, behavioral problems, and parental psychiatric disorder. A third domain may be the dieting vulnerability domain. It examines dieting risk related to family and family history of eating disorders, obesity or obesity risks.

Significant limitations of this approach concern the potential influence of retrospective recall bias. However, other sources of data, such as medical charts, can be used which might enhance the reliability and validity of these retrospective longitudinal methodologies. Even still, the endemic challenges with the follow-back approach make the alternative, follow-up approach as the more common of the two methodologies.

The prospective follow-up investigation is used to follow groups in the highest risk age group and look for variances in those who develop eating disorders and those that do not.

One such longitudinal study took a group of girls and boys and studied them from grade seven through ten. The domains of vulnerability examined were substance-related impulsivity, development (physical and cognitive), and negative affect or attitudes. The students completed self-report assessments of eating disorder symptoms, mood disturbances, self-esteem, dieting, exercise, body image, personality, and other risky behaviors.

In this study, negative affect/attitudes, which included body dissatisfaction, depression, emotionality such as unhappiness or anxiety, ineffectiveness and interceptive awareness (recognition of various feelings and internal sensations), were highly significant predictors of the onset of disordered eating attitudes and behaviors in both sexes. The authors of this study associated this with an idealization of body image for both girls and boys of this age prevalent in the media.

Prospective studies such as this, however, require large samples, time and are costly to conduct. For this reason, they are less commonly used in research within this area.

Experimental Research

Experimental research studies are another method often used. In these, an independent variable is manipulated causing a change in a dependent variable. These methods are designed to identify potential causal factors in the development of disordered eating.

The issue with this method has to do with the ethics of causing an eating disorder or disordered eating behaviors. For this reason, the researchers often use analogue studies. They begin with a premise concerning the factors that cause eating disorders and then test the impact of these factors on the eating-related attitudes or behaviors of college undergraduates, for example.

As an illustration, researchers may hypothesize that dieting causes binge eating. They can then compare the responses of students whose scores on dietary restraint assessments are high with those that were low. Those with high scores could be called the "dieters" and those with low scores could be identified as "non-dieters." Half of each group is then told to drink a milkshake while the other half drinks nothing (the independent variable), and then both groups are given the opportunity to take part in a "taste test" where they are presented with a variety of foods to sample (the dependent variable). Results of studies such as these have shown that the dieters ate much more food during the taste test, as compared to the non-dieters, even when they'd just consumed a milkshake, suggesting that dieting was the pre-potent factor that predicted subsequent eating.

Clinical Experimental Studies

Another experimental method is the clinical experimental study. In one such study tryptophan levels were manipulated in two groups of women. Tryptophan is the biological precursor to serotonin, which plays a large function in clients with eating disorders. Two groups of women were used, one with eating disorders and one group without. Half of the women (equal numbers form each group) were given a healthy drink and the other half a drink that was tryptophan-depleted. All participants were given rating scales to determine mood. The women also kept food diaries for 24 hours.

The results showed that all of the women who drank the tryptophan-depleted drink showed reduced levels of tryptophan, but only those who had been diagnosed with BN exhibited increased dysphoria or dissatisfaction with life and more loss of control over eating than the control group who drank the same drink.

Naturalistic Investigations

A further method often used to research eating disorders is naturalistic investigation.

Naturalistic studies rely on the investigation of naturally occurring groups or events. The study of prisoners of war in concentration camps and among WWII combat veterans would be an example. Studies such as these have found distinct relationships between starvation and binge eating. Other examples of naturalistic studies include twin studies, or adoption studies, that similarly look to determine the role of nature (i.e., genetic factors) and nurture (i.e., environmental factors) in the development of disordered eating.

Research Conclusion

Longitudinal research, experimental designs, correlational studies, and naturalistic design are all methods of research used in the study of eating disorders. The most common methods, however, are correlational studies that examine the relationship between a variety of factors and aspects of disordered eating. Including greater diversity within the samples studies, as well as the methods utilized, will accelerate an understanding of the causes and correlates of disordered eating.

CHAPTER 9

Psychological Treatments and Cognitive Behavioral Therapies

*R*ebecca was defiant about needing help for her anorexia. Whenever her parents brought up the issue of her eating habits, she didn't react well. She vehemently denied having a problem, saying, "I'm fine," or "Don't be ridiculous."

It was not easy to get Rebecca to her appointment with the eating disorder specialist. Her parents had to be very firm.

In their initial visits, there were tears before and distress during. When they got home, Rebecca would disappear into her room. Her mom could understand that Rebecca didn't like what the doctor had made her understand, but he did know about eating disorders, and knew that her avoidance of certain issues was a significant part of her problem. During the sessions, he took in his stride her frequently nasty behavior. Anorexia is about avoiding confrontation and conflict, which was exactly what Rebecca was doing. So the therapy was critical to her overcoming her efforts to build a wall around herself.

Rebecca and her parents all participated in the therapy. Her mom and dad spoke with the doctor together, and then Rebecca and her sister met with him separately. At the time, Rebecca's relationship with her younger sister was also quite strained and even heated.

The doctor didn't say a lot during the initial sessions with Rebecca, but sat and let the family talk. At the beginning, this was uncomfortable and a very unusual situation for the family. Over time, they became more at ease.

The discussions were very empowering. The doctor was very principled and committed, and didn't hesitate to tell Rebecca she was being rude or provide her parents with clear suggestions about helping keep Rebecca at home. If they had a bad week with Rebecca, a half-hour meeting with the doctor would leave them with a better grip on the situation.

His advice and the consequences he set in response to Rebecca's behavior were simple but very effective.

At home, her parents showed their daughter "tough love," and they home schooled her. Once Rebecca gained some weight and was allowed to go back to school, she decided that she was happier at school than at home. However, it wasn't easy for her to change her behavior. Her parents managed to get through to her in the home situation, but her outpatient therapy remained very important.

They had to be united and be firm, especially on Rebecca's bad days, which could involve explosive outbursts and very abusive behavior from her. She would also be manipulative and deceitful, so it was really important that both her mom and dad were fully involved and aware of Rebecca's behavior all the time.

Treatments for eating disorders often involve medical as well a psychological and behavioral therapies. Although many people never seek help of any kind, for those who do seek treatment, it can restore them back to normal eating patterns and bring them back to a healthy lifestyle.

The data that have been collected through various studies indicate that men are just as likely as women to complete inpatient treatment, though men do not follow through as well with outpatient treatment.

Studies reveal that patients who suffer from anorexia nervosa reach out for support much more often than patients with bulimia nervosa.

Due to space issues, many patients are put on a waitlist and continue in outpatient care when they really require an inpatient program. Residential treatment is similar to inpatient treatment. Residential services can be private, for-profit or not-for-profit, and establish their own programs for treatment and determine their own desired outcomes for discharge or termination.

Patients with eating disorders who do get admitted to inpatient facilities sometimes find the conditions are highly controlled and can feel confrontational. Because most who are admitted for inpatient care are severely malnourished, it can become necessary to force changes in the unhealthy eating habits the patients have acquired. Weight, food intake and blood levels are monitored on an ongoing basis.

Patients often find the treatment difficult because they are so accustomed to concealing their issues. Discharge from such a facility usually is accompanied by a healthy weight gain and maintenance of the healthier eating habits among anorectic patients. This in itself is what gets most patients on board with the program. They want to be discharged. Along with individual therapy, group therapy sessions and journal writing are used to help bring each person to healthier place, both mentally and physically.

The overall effectiveness of the treatment for eating disorders is not always easy to determine in actual clinical settings. Patients are discharged at different points when they achieve a wide variety of different outcomes. Some release a patient when they no longer are medically unstable, without regard to their psychological condition. Others consider particular levels of weight gain, often determined by the patients' body mass index (BMI).

One of the reasons residential and inpatient treatment data are difficult to assess is because the patients are not randomly distributed across different kinds of standardized treatments. Instead, they are treated specifically for the individual's need. While this idiosyncratic treatment, tailored to the individual needs of each patient, is widely regarded as good practice, it introduces significant variability into the treatment programs, making it difficult to determine the intensity or specific components of treatment that contribute most to treatment success.

Psychcoeducation

Psychoeducation is the beginning of the treatment processes and it guides the direction of the treatment. It is based in helping the patients understand their conditions, their contributing factors and their treatment options. It involves education about the psychology of the disease. Patients are made to focus on their idealization of thinness, including its accuracy and implications.

As an example, patients might be invited to consider what becoming "thin" might say about them or bring to them in their life or their relationships. Often this sort of exercise exposes a range of distorted beliefs that follow from the idealization of thinness. The patient's education also stresses that the body has defenses against starvation and goes into survival mode by shutting down parts of the functioning in the body to save on calories. Patients learn how their body copes with starvation, how unnatural it is, and how it eventually leads to death if not corrected. This education about the disease is not designed as a standalone intervention, but rather as a prelude to subsequent therapy that is designed to promote attitudinal, emotional, and behavioral change.

Psychodynamic Therapy

Psychodynamic therapy is a specific method used in regular sessions with a therapist. In this type of therapy the goal is often to allow the patient to explore with the therapist the reasons for their thinking and behaviors. In the beginning, most talk revolves around the symptoms of the underlying disease. The patients will talk about how eating makes them feel, how they feel fat and unworthy and how these behaviors and thoughts are related to some anxiety or stress or trauma. It can take a long time for the patient to get to this point. This kind of treatment often explores the past and connects the patients' past experience with underlying causes on the one hand, or contemporary triggers, on the other, for the eating disorder. Because psychodynamic therapy is often combined with other therapies at the same time it is difficult to yield any conclusive data regarding its effectiveness as a standalone intervention. This kind of approach is often called a non-directive approach in it is guided more by the experience of the patient than it is directed by the objectives of the therapist or a predetermined therapeutic process or outcome.

Cognitive-Behavioral Therapies

Cognitive-behavioral therapy works to disrupt the negative body image thoughts and related rituals. Cognitive-behavioral therapies are more structured and directive techniques. These do not explore previous traumas in one's life, but rather tend to concentrate on contemporary thoughts, feelings and behaviors, and the relationship among them.

Education is the first stage of treatment. The first part of this therapy is based on helping the patients to examine their thoughts and beliefs about being fat or thin, and to assess the accuracy and implications of those thoughts and beliefs.

Patients are commonly required to do three things in particular.

First, they must go out and view people in public who seem to be in happy relationships regardless of their weight.

Second, they are challenged regarding their beliefs about how being thin is essential to bringing them love. The intervention pursues the idea that if a person would love you merely for your thinness, that may not be the strongest basis for a relationship or a genuine valuing of the patient as a person.

The third part is to explore relationships and people who the patient cares about and loves, yet who are not thin.

Getting the individual to focus on these three issues is a pathway toward changing potentially limiting body images and the beliefs or attitudes that accompany them. Cognitive-behavioral therapies often require patients to self-monitor their eating, as well as all inappropriate compensatory (i.e. vomiting, exercise, use of diuretics) or coping behaviors, by recording them in a journal. They are prescribed a regular pattern of eating at least three meals per day with snacks and learn to eat frequently. Stimulus controls must be identified, acknowledged and written down. All of this work is designed to educate the patients about the disease, about themselves, and about their relationship with the world.

In the second part of this program, patients are taught to identify their problematic and distorted thinking, to describe it, and to find alternative responses to it. For example, if they catch themselves saying, "If I get fat, no one will love me," then they write that thought down and examine it rationally. It is true, for example, that some people may have negative stereotypes about overweight people, but most overweight people are in constructive, loving relationships and are loved for who they are, regardless of what their weight or weight fluctuations may be.

As a result of reviewing their distorted thought, the patient can then re-structure it into a more rational thought that better fits the contours of reality. So, for example, they might say, "If I become large it may trigger some negative stereotypes in some people, but what I want is a loving relationship with someone who loves me for who I am, and many, many large people are in relationships like that."

The third and final stage is to work on maintenance and progression of a healthy lifestyle. Patients continue to use their journaling, learn to understand the difference between a lapse and the full return to the disorder, and they are given homework assignments that focus on problem solving.

Interpersonal Therapy

Another kind of therapy is interpersonal therapy. It is similar to cognitive-behavior therapy but with the focus on relationships.

There are three stages.

The first is learning to identify the problems or triggers of their eating disorders–for example, what triggers a binge or a purging episode. When doing this, a patient has to examine previous conditions or relationships that are connected with the disturbed eating. Often, interpersonal turmoil triggers emotional upset (e.g. anxiety, anger, self-loathing) that then triggers efforts to self-punish or self-sooth through eating-related behaviors. They must learn to understand the patterns of behaviors that they use to cope with problems.

The second step is to focus on the specific problems that seem to trigger the bulimia and address those directly through assertiveness training, conflict management, or relaxation training. Patients learn to express their feelings constructively rather than burying them inside and dealing with them indirectly through destructive eating-related behaviors.

The third part of this therapy is the repeated rehearsal and application of the new relationship-oriented skills until the patient has mastered them and can apply them independently in real-life situations.

In interpersonal therapy, after the first session, weight and eating become background issues while interpersonal and emotional issues are addressed in greater detail. The focus is to steer toward identifying and working through relationship problems. In recent years there has been a crossover of interpersonal therapy with cognitive-behavioral therapy, which shows promise in the treatment of eating disorders.

Dialectical Behavior Therapy (DBT)

Dialectical behavior therapy (DBT) is another promising treatment for disordered eating. Dialectical behavior therapy was initially used in individuals with personality disorders but has shown a positive effect with those who have eating disorders.

A "dialectic" refers to an integration of synthesis of opposites. In the case of dialectical behavior therapy, one of the dialectics is between acceptance and reactivity.

The theory behind the approach is that some people are prone to react in a more intense and out-of-the-ordinary manner toward certain emotional situations, primarily those found in romantic, family, and friend relationships. DBT theory suggests that some people's arousal levels in such situations can increase far more quickly than the average person's, attain a higher level of emotional stimulation, and take a significant amount of time to return to baseline arousal levels. This therapy then uses a variety of strategies to enable and enhance acceptance in preference to reaction in the face of powerful emotions. Many of the techniques encourage mindfulness, distress tolerance, interpersonal effectiveness, and emotional regulation. The notion is that if the patient learns to deal with his or her powerful negative emotions more constructively, rather than reactively, they can prevent the use of disturbed eating as a mechanism for the expression, control, or modulation of their feelings.

Family-Based Therapy

For individuals still living with parents, family therapy is recommended. Family therapy recognizes the interpersonal, often familial context in which disturbed eating is often generated and/or perpetuated. Often, the patient has experienced food or appearance-related evaluations or judgments on the part of one or more family members. And equally often, the efforts of family members to help can actually wind up hurting. So family members are guided through the process of coming to understand their own (often unwitting) contributions to the disturbed eating, and to accept responsibility for changing their behavior, often to a more accepting, supportive role. Repositioning family members to be "on the patient's" side rather than "on their case" is often one objective of family therapy, where the target of the therapeutic interventions is concentrated less on the patients and/or their thinking than on the family interactions and relationships that can provide and support constructive change.

Building on the reported need and support from caregivers or family, increased family-based therapy (FBT) and couple therapy using cognitive-behavioral methods have shown promise. These systemic interventions can increase positive communication and relational aspects in the daily life of a recovering AN patient. By teaching the caregiver about the disorder, what happens neurologically and biologically, they are able to relate more favorably to the anorectic individual. Given vital information on how to reduce anxiety and stress by learning more about the AN individual helps caregivers to become more empathetic and to reduce those feelings of frustration or criticism that tend to put the AN patient at risk.

Recent studies of the neurobiological effects on the AN patient suggest that extreme negative temperament traits do contribute to the disease and these traits can be managed by behavioral therapy, especially with the assistance of the family or caregiver. This focus on both higher levels of awareness and constructive management techniques has been well accepted by both the anorectic and the caregiver.

Gestalt Therapy

A humanistic approach to psychotherapy, Gestalt therapy is based in the belief that people are born to be spontaneous and whole within themselves but as they build more relationships they lose this sense of self. In treatment the therapists will bypass rational thinking processes and directly address emotional states of the client. "The empty chair" is a famous technique for doing this kind of therapy. The client will visualize a part of what they are missing or a person they feel has control over them and then they talk to the empty chair. It is an effort for the client to regain control over his or her whole self. The belief is that the whole of a person is more than the sum of his or her parts. In the context of disordered eating, the use of Gestalt therapy might be directed at identifying and integrating parts of the self in a way that builds greater self-awareness and acceptance.

Classic Psychoanalysis

While classic psychoanalysisis a not common therapeutic approach for treating disordered eating, many neo-analytic approaches are still used. In these therapies, internal conflicts are identified and exposed, with the idea that these represent the underlying causes of the eating disorders. Gaining insight and understanding of these causes allows the eating disordered person to address these underlying causes directly. When this is done the patient should be able to feel a satisfaction and completeness that the past issues are resolved so that they can move forward without interference from those unresolved issues.

The National Eating Disorder Association (NEDA) produces materials, screening tools, and they raise money to support research and treatment of eating disorders. NEDA is supported by the American Psychiatric Association, American Psychological Association, American Academy of Pediatrics, and the National Collegiate Athletic Association. They all recommend regular mental health checkups along with regular physical health checkups. Awareness is ever increasing and the money for research and study has taken a more public and political stage in recent years. There is hope, many people working toward a cure, and growing support for those who suffer with these conditions.

Other Interventions

Beyond psychotherapies, a range of other interventions can be helpful with disordered eating.

Nutritional counseling and medication, for example, can be used to increase healthy choices and decrease anxiety.

Behavioral weight loss programs offer the benefit of psychotherapy and healthy eating.

A newer therapy is called the acceptance and commitment therapy (ACT). It focuses on the inner turmoil of normal life and how to move forward in more positive ways instead of choosing unhealthy methods. Studies show it can be effective in the treatment of disordered eating. It uses education, changing thought processes, and working through the issues.

Other therapies are used in conjunction with the more established paths.

Expressive therapy uses the arts to bring out the feelings of those with eating disorder disease. Dance, drama, painting, drawing, and music can offer alternative ways to communicate.

Light therapy for those who might be affected with seasonal affective disorder can create a positive effect on some individuals.

The most important part of any treatment is the integration of healthy eating, changing behavioral responses to difficult situations, education regarding the thoughts that govern a person's negative self-worth, and treatment for medical conditions and for the underlying anxiety or other mental illness. There is no one, single method that is best for everyone. It takes a team of professionals to work together to build a structure of management that is controlled until the patient is well enough to take over.

The goal in treatment is to resolve the feelings of hopelessness and despair. In order for this to happen it requires behavior, cognitive, and sometimes medication therapies. The use of medication often can improve the effectiveness of the various psychotherapeutic treatments by addressing underlying issues of depression or anxiety that can exacerbate the disordered eating.

Treatment for Addictive Disorders

Treatment for eating disorders is often coupled with treatment of addictive disorders. Individuals who suffer from underlying mental illness will often seek out addictive habits or chemicals that calm them for the moment. The inappropriate eating, the unhealthy search for coping mechanisms and strategies for hiding and manipulation of people and situations creates habits that take years to unravel in therapy. The treatments that work for one does not necessarily work for another. Some find success and some do not.

Education of the medical communities, school counselors, teachers, and others who are around youth and children could become the first form of intervention. Teaching children and teens about how to cope with problems, who is there to support them and where they can go for help is the second line of defense in treating eating disorders.

Temperament Patterns

So-called temperament-based treatment for anorexia nervosa is fairly new but the focus has been on behavioral strategies that the patient and the caregiver could learn in order to recognize their temperament patterns and help to develop strategies that build recovery and positive coping strategies. This method was developed after patients reported that the relationship between the caregiver and themselves was key to their recovery. Studies have also shown that a focus on the development of constructive coping strategies is beneficial. Data supports this as patients have reported that during recovery, they tended to eat the same foods at the same times each day. Their way of coping in more positive ways included avoidance of the choices of what or when to eat, which can generate anxiety. Instead, they reduced the uncertainty surrounding the selection of food and created rules to structure their food intake. This is one way individuals with anorexia nervosa manage in more successful ways.

Temperament-Based Treatments

Recent neurobiological models of AN have determined that the personality, ego or temperament characteristics do greatly contribute to the development and treatment pathways for the disease. Knowing which mechanism to target comes from observable traits. These temperament-based treatments for anorexia nervosa (TBT-AN) guide the professionals and provide improved results. Much of the treatment of eating disorders includes addressing the anxiety, altering reward sensitivity, and overcoming deficits in awareness and interpretation of bodily cues. Such treatment involves awareness of their emotions and their bodies, and learning positive, appropriate and constructive methods to manage their targeted behaviors. This is the opposite of trying to change the temperament. Instead, it recruits the use of their native temperament into the treatment and its interventions. Obsessiveness can become an ally, for example, by directing it to the detection of false thinking or distorted body images or the perceived reactions of others.

CHAPTER 10

Medications and Hospitalization

In 2014, researchers Elsa J. Kracke and Aneesh K. Tosh described a female college student—whom we'll call "Joan"—who suffered with anorexia nervosa over her four-year undergraduate career. In their paper, "Treatment of anorexia nervosa with long-term risperidone in an outpatient setting: case study," they noted there are currently few studies focusing on the efficacy of long-term atypical antipsychotics to treat anorexia nervosa in the pediatric population. The authors noted that previous studies on anorexia nervosa treatment had occurred during inpatient treatment and had limited follow-up due to patients' refusal to initiate or maintain medication compliance.

Joan's story began at the beginning of her freshman year of college, when she presented herself at her university health clinic with an established diagnosis of anorexia nervosa. She weighed about ninety pounds. Joan's eating disorder had started by her restricting her consumption of fats, progressing to eliminating all fats, and then reducing overall calories. These characteristics were consistent with anorexia nervosa restrictive subtype. She did not report purging, laxative abuse, or excessive exercising to compensate for calorie intake. Although Joan had played competitive tennis in high school, during college she considerably reduced her level of activity.

She noted anxiety and fatigue while denying signs of depression. No significant past medical history, surgical history, or family history, including history of eating disorders or other psychiatric conditions, was mentioned during her treatment. Her medication list when she presented consisted of escitalopram (an antidepressant of the selective serotonin reuptake inhibitor class), doxycycline for acne, a generic multivitamin, and a fish oil supplement.

Due to her low weight, the multidisciplinary medical team—her physician, a dietitian, and a therapist—made the decision for her to enter residential treatment at an outside eating disorder treatment facility. After three months of structured inpatient treatment, her weight increased to 104 pounds and she was able to enroll in classes for the spring semester.

Over the next ten months she had no significant improvement in weight or mealtime anxiety. Escitalopram was discontinued and replaced with sertraline, another antidepressant. To treat her anxiety, the dose of sertraline gradually increased over a one-year period. Throughout this time, at meal times Joan still had subjective feelings of anxiety and rigidity (refusal to eat), and therefore did not have significant improvement in weight gain.

After nearly three years of treatment in college, at a weight of 101 pounds, Joan agreed to begin a low-dose atypical antipsychotic, risperidone. Approximately three months later, having gained only three pounds and reporting no medication adverse side effects, the dose of risperidone was increased. After seven months of compliance at this higher dose, she gained another thirteen pounds and was able to decrease her sertraline dose.

In response to the drug, Joan expressed a greater willingness to eat, her weight improved, and she had resumption of menses. She was compliant with treatment and maintained her weight gain.

In the spring of her senior year, Joan's weight remained stable, and the last weight recorded in in college was 115 pounds. After graduation her care was transferred from university, and she continued to remain in recovery.

Near the end of her treatment, after resumption of menses, Joan was queried as to why she felt the risperidone was helpful in her recovery. The patient felt that after starting the risperidone, during meal times she felt more interested in eating. Despite having similar motivation to improve her nutrition in the past, her mealtime rigidity was a barrier that she was not able to overcome until the risperidone was started. It happens to be well known that a side effect of risperidone therapy is weight gain. While her metabolic labs were normal and stable during her treatment, the possibility that weight gain as a side effect of risperidone contributed to her resumption of menses is another conceivable factor in her recovery. Therefore, a combination of factors related to the risperidone likely played a role Joan's recovery.

In this case, Joan had decreased rigid thinking, measurable weight gain, and resolution of secondary amenorrhea without apparent medication side effects. Researchers concluded that the atypical antipsychotic risperidone may be an effective long-term outpatient treatment option for patients with anorexia nervosa.

Medications

We live in a world where prescription medications have become ubiquitous.

In the United States, the national average for the number of drug prescriptions written per person per year is about twelve. Among children eighteen and younger—those who are most susceptible to beginning an eating disorder—the number is four per person. The rate climbs with age, until people in their eighties are written an astonishing average of twenty-nine prescriptions per person.

In the face of his growing rate of medication, many health care experts believe that the answer to disease does not always come from a pill. They urge that medications be used only as a last resort, and not as the reflexive response of a doctor seeking to provide his or her patient with immediate relief from their ailment.

It is against this backdrop that medical professionals must carefully weigh the pros and cons of using medications to treat an eating disorder.

On the subject of medications for eating disorders, opinions are mixed.

On its website, the Mayo Clinic says flatly, "No medications are approved to treat anorexia because none has been found to work very well. However, antidepressants or other psychiatric medications can help treat other mental disorders you may also have, such as depression or anxiety." This doesn't directly address the issue of whether the "other" disorder such as depression can be a causative agent of an eating disorder, and therefore treating the "other" disorder can be instrumental in resolving the eating disorder itself.

Many health care practitioners believe medication can be a valuable tool in the treatment of eating disorders. However, it is important that a treatment plan also include some form of psychotherapy and nutritional counseling. Medication alone can't cure an eating disorder the way an aspirin can cure a headache. However, medications such as antidepressants and anti-anxiety medications may help with symptoms of depression or anxiety, which are frequently associated with eating disorders. Medications may also help the patient control urges to binge or purge or to manage excessive preoccupations with food and diet.

Anorexia Nervosa

Compared to other eating disorders, medication is used less frequently to treat anorexia. When medication is called for, as in Joan's case, antidepressants are typically prescribed to treat underlying mental health problems.

In their 2005 paper "Pharmacological Treatment of Eating Disorders," Kiranmai Gorla and Maju Mathews noted that at that time, the guidelines of the American Psychological Association (APA) stated that psychotropic medications should not be used as the sole or primary treatment for anorexia nervosa, but they can be considered for the prevention of relapse in weight restored patients or to treat depression or obsessive compulsive disorder.

There is some evidence that antidepressants may help maintain weight gain in successfully treated patients. Anxiolytic medications may be helpful before meals for the anorexic patient who is having anxiety before eating. Several reports have been published in which olanzapine was successfully used in patients with severe anorexia nervosa for stimulating appetite and weight gain.

Fluoxetine (marketed by Eli Lilly as Prozac) may help people with anorexia overcome their depression and maintain a healthy weight once they have gotten their weight and eating under control. Fluoxetine is in a class of drugs called selective serotonin uptake inhibitors (SSRIs). These drugs increase serotonin levels, a brain chemical connected to mood. If the patient does not do well on an SSRI, doctors may prescribe olanzapine (Zyprexa), an antipsychotic drug typically used to treat schizophrenia. This medication has been found to help some people with anorexia gain weight and change their obsessive thinking.

Atypical antipsychotics are emerging as a treatment option in the management of anorexia nervosa. For eating disorders, **risperidone** has not been studied as frequently as **olanzapine**, an atypical antipsychotic approved by the U.S. Food and Drug Administration (FDA) for the treatment of schizophrenia and bipolar disorder.

In 2004, Timothy D. Brewerton noted that olanzapine's propensity toward enhanced appetite and weight gain, as well as its antianxiety, antiobsessional, and antidepressant properties makes it theoretically an excellent drug for AN, especially the restricting subtype. It also increases sleep and decreases motor activity, thereby conserving energy expenditure. Open trials and case reports have been promising. Adult patients often resist or refuse to take olanzapine because of its weight gain and soporific effects; however, in children and adolescents, parents can ensure compliance. Very low doses are usually sufficient to attain the desired effect.

Lithium has been shown in one controlled trial to be statistically better than placebo in a small group of patients being treated at the National Institute of Mental Health on an intensive, highly structured, specialized treatment unit. As described by Brewerton in 2004, the effect was small. Eating disorder specialists generally deem the potential risks of lithium treatment in this population to be far greater than the possible benefits, largely due to the danger of lithium toxicity secondary to dehydration and electrolyte imbalances from starvation, compulsive exercising, and/or purging.

Another study found **amitriptyline** (trade name Elavil) statistically better than placebo for patients who were both bulimic and anorexic, while **cyproheptadine** (Periactin) was better for restricting anorexia. However, other studies have had mixed results.

Bulimia Nervosa

Accumulating evidence suggests that antidepressants in combination with psychotherapy can be effective in the treatment of bulimia nervosa.

Even if they aren't depressed, people with bulimia often respond well to SSRI antidepressants.

Gorla and Mathews, as well as other researchers, have reported that a number of studies have confirmed the efficacy of various medications in the treatment of bulimia.

Fluoxetine, the only antidepressant approved by the U.S. Food and Drug Administration to treat bulimia, can help people stop binging and purging when used alone or with CBT. The evidence for the use of fluoxetine in the treatment of bulimia nervosa comes in the form of various case reports, systematic studies, and double-blind, randomized placebo controlled trials. In a double-blind, placebo-controlled study by Halmi, et al., 382 patients were randomly assigned to receive fluoxetine or placebo for eight weeks. Treatment with a lower dose of fluoxetine resulted in reductions in binge eating and vomiting compared with placebo. Those receiving a higher dose of fluoxetine had even greater improvement, with a 67% reduction in binge eating and a 56% reduction in vomiting.

Tricyclic antidepressants, such as desipramine (marketed by Aventis as Norpramin), imipramine (marketed by Ciba Geigy as Tofranil,), and amitriptyline (marketed by Merck & Co. as Elavil), have been found to be effective.

Monoamine oxidase inhibitors have been found to be more effective than placebo in decreasing the binging and vomiting in patients with bulimia nervosa.

Buspirone (marketed by Bristol Myers Squibb as Buspar) has been effective in decreasing binging and vomiting in patients with bulimia nervosa. However, studies with lithium did not find it to be effective in the treatment of bulimia nervosa.

The anticonvulsant topiramate (marketed by Ortho-McNeil Pharmaceutical as Topomax) may help people with bulimia suppress their urge to binge and reduce their preoccupation with eating and weight. However, topiramate can have more adverse side effects than the SSRIs.

Administered in a randomized study of outpatients with binge eating disorder (not bulimia nervosa), topiramate significantly reduced binge frequency (94% vs. 46%) and showed a weight loss of 13 pounds versus 2.6 pounds. However, a large percentage of patients in both the topiramate and placebo groups did not complete the full fourteen weeks of treatment.

Ondansetron (marketed by GlaxoSmithKline as Zofran), an anti-emetic medication, is also reported to reduce binge eating and self-induced vomiting in a small placebo-controlled study of patients with bulimia nervosa.

Other SSRI antidepressants may be helpful in treating bulimia and are often used, although scientific studies to support their use are limited.

Clinical experience supports the use of most selective serotonin reuptake inhibitors (i.e., fluoxetine, sertraline and citalopram) as well as some of the newer antidepressants (i.e., venlafaxine).

Binge Eating

The standard treatment for binge eating, as well as other eating disorders, usually involves a combination of counseling and psychotherapy. Some doctors also prescribe antidepressants to try and curb eating disorders, though they are not approved for that use. (This is so-called "off-label" use.) Evidence suggests that antidepressants can help treat binge eating disorder. SSRIs, such as fluoxetine (Prozac) and sertraline (Zoloft), may help reduce binge eating and can improve mood in patients who are also struggling with depression or anxiety.

Antidepressants in general are not effective in weight reduction.

Some doctors have also tried anticonvulsants (topiramate) for treating binge-eating disorder. Vyvanse, known chemically as lisdexamfetamine dimesylate, is part of a family of drugs that stimulate the central nervous system.

Federal health regulators have approved an attention deficit disorder drug for treatment for binge-eating disorder. The Food and Drug Administration originally approved Vyvanse in 2007 as a once-a-day pill for attention deficit hyperactivity disorder. In February of 2015, the agency approved the drug for adults who compulsively overeat. The drug is not approved for weight loss.

Hospitalization

If the life of the person with an eating disorder is in immediate danger, he or she may need treatment in a hospital emergency room for such issues as a heart rhythm disturbance, dehydration, electrolyte imbalances or psychiatric problems. Hospitalization may be required for medical complications, psychiatric emergencies, severe malnutrition or continued refusal to eat. Hospitalization may be on a medical or psychiatric ward.

Some clinics specialize in treating people with eating disorders. Some may offer day programs or residential programs rather than full hospitalization. Specialized eating disorder programs may offer more intensive treatment over longer periods of time.

Because of the host of complications anorexia causes, the patient may need frequent monitoring of vital signs, hydration level and electrolytes, as well as related physical conditions. In severe cases, people with anorexia may initially require feeding through a tube that's placed in their nose and goes to the stomach (nasogastric tube).

A primary care doctor may be the one who coordinates care with the other health care professionals involved. Sometimes, though, it's the mental health provider who coordinates care.

The Society for Adolescent Medicine has published guidelines for hospitalization. According to their guidelines, one or more of the following criteria justify hospitalization:

- Severe malnutrition (weight less than 75 percent of average body weight for age, sex, and height).
- Dehydration.
- Electrolyte disturbances (hypokalemia, hyponatremia, hypophosphatemia).
- Cardiac dysrhythmia.
- Physiologic instability, such as severe bradycardia (heart rate less than 50 beats per minute during the day or less than 45 at night), hypotension (less than 80/50mmHg), hypothermia (less than 96° F), orthostatic changes in pulse (more than 20 beats per minute) or blood pressure (more than 10 mmHg).
- Arrested growth and development.
- Failure of outpatient treatment.
- Acute food refusal.
- Uncontrollable binging and purging.
- Acute medical complication of malnutrition (e.g., syncope, seizures, cardiac failure, pancreatitis, etc.).
- Acute psychiatric emergencies (e.g., suicidal ideation, acute psychosis).
- Comorbid diagnosis that interferes with the treatment of eating disorders (e.g., severe depression, obsessive compulsive disorder, severe family dysfunction).

The guidelines published by the APA are similar but emphasize psychiatric and behavioral factors along with medical factors.

The choice between medical or psychiatric hospitalization is based on resources available, medical condition, and age of the patient. Whether it is a psychiatric unit or a medical unit, the hospital unit must have experience in treating this special population and should have guidelines and protocols in place. A caring and experienced team comprising a medical doctor, a psychiatrist, nurses, a dietitian, and a therapist are very important for any successful treatment of eating disorder patients.

The first goal of treatment is getting back to a healthy weight. A person can't recover from an eating disorder without restoring an appropriate weight and learning proper nutrition. While in the care of an inpatient facility, if the patient is able to eat the prescribed amount consistently, he or she may be allowed to choose what foods they would like to eat at meals. However, if they are not able to eat enough at meals, they may be required to use meal supplements.

If the patient can't eat enough to regain or maintain weight, doctors and other treatment team members may recommend medical refeeding, which involves inserting a feeding tube through the patient's nose down into the stomach.

Another form of support that inpatient hospitalization is able to provide is supported meals, in which a staff member will typically eat all meals with the patient. The goal is to provide support and monitor intake. The staff member is available before and after meals to process any urges that the patient is experiencing and to support the patient during these anxiety-provoking times.

The patient should remain in the hospital until his or her physical condition stabilizes, mental status improves, and a care plan is in place. Unfortunately, the managed care health system does not always allow this. One study looked into the outcomes after hospitalization and found that those eating disorder patients who remained in the hospital until they had regained adequate weight (90%–92% of ideal body weight) had a better outcome compared with those who did not regain adequate weight. These findings support the argument for adequate length of stay in the hospital for the successful treatment of eating disorders.

If continued hospitalization isn't necessary, the patient may be moved into a day treatment program that has been designed to complement and extend the inpatient program's structure and therapeutic care. It can also be very useful for individuals who don't necessarily require inpatient hospitalization but could benefit from a more intensive level of care than outpatient therapy can provide. A day treatment program can provide the important elements of structure and therapy throughout the day, balanced with the reassurance of returning home each evening. During their independent time away from the unit, patients are expected to practice newly developed coping skills and self-care while nurturing a commitment to their recovery outside of the hospital.

CHAPTER 11

Nutrition and Eating Disorders

*C*arol's ten-year-old son, Stanley, is causing significant stress for the family and Carol. Carol revealed he has always been a "picky eater," from the early age of three years old, only accepting a limited number of food items, such as McDonald's chicken nuggets, bacon and mashed potatoes. At ten years of age, his food choices have not differentiated or matured. His diet consists of less than ten food items, some requiring very precise ways of preparation. Carol says her son will eat cereal, grilled cheese on white bread, melted cheese on white buns, melted cheese on breakfast biscuits, cheese pizza, French fries, mashed potatoes and corn. Carol says her son's eating habits are ruining meal time for their family and causing a lot of problems.

Carol continued to discuss how they are unable to go out with friends to a restaurant because Stanley will sometimes "throw a fit" when he can't find anything on the menu to eat. Some restaurants will make Stanley a grilled cheese sandwich, even if it is not on the menu. However, if Stanley believes for any reason the grilled cheese was made on the same grill as the meat he will refuse to eat it. Carol admitted she sometimes makes a special trip to get Stanley his own meal through the drive-thru for him, while the rest of the family eats somewhere else. Carol acknowledged she feels guilty when she denies him what he wants because she does not want him to be hungry.

Stanley reported other foods make him "feel sick" and they "look gross" so he doesn't want to eat them. When asked what other foods he had tried, he replied, "I don't want anything else because I just know it will be awful!" Carol says visits to the doctor have *not been helpful, as there appears to be nothing medically wrong with her son. She has brought him to the clinic to see if counseling may be a solution.*

The counselor recommended family counseling as a way to target both the child's fear of food and "picky eating," as well as the mother's distress and anxiety surrounding the issue. The counselor included psychoeducational information to assist Carol with learning how decreasing her own anxiety would, in turn, decrease her son's. The counselor also worked with Carol on identifying her own anxiety triggers related to the feeding issues, which included: fear and judgment of others, avoiding a tantrum, Stanley's nutritional needs and whether or not she was using the "right" approach.

Encouraging Stanley to broaden his food choices involved more education and training with Carol. The counselor worked with Carol to develop a menu plan that included Stanley's "safe" foods, while also incorporating dishes Carol and the rest of the family might desire. Carol is instructed and encouraged to serve both Stanley's foods and the other foods together and reduce pressuring Stanley to eat anything he does not want to eat. The counselor also worked with Carol on finding ways to make feeding-time fun and foods exciting, as well as inventive.

Nutritional Challenges and Eating Disorders

Not surprisingly, many people with eating disorders also have nutritional challenges and deficiencies. Once in treatment, a major part of the program is nutrition counseling on a one-to-one basis. A nutritional counselor provides information about the basic food groups and healthy eating, and also helps to plan meals, work on attitudes about food and weight, and build relationships to gain trust.

The first job of the nutritional therapist is to learn as much about the patient as possible; eating habits, how long the dieting has been going on and key information about their family eating patterns and expectations. Knowing habits of the patient's environment, likes and dislikes, activities enjoyed, exercising and other personal aspects of the life of an eating disordered person can help the nutritionist come up with a workable plan for the patient. The center of the nutritional counseling is focused on balanced meals, eating from all food groups, understanding portion sizes and how the body needs and uses nutrients. Teaching about the food pyramid, the need for proteins, carbohydrates and fats for body fuel and good health are important. The client has to rebuild a healthy relationship with food, which can involve powerful emotional and psychological issues, given that they often will have experienced a love-hate relationship with food and longstanding struggles regarding control in relation to it.

The Effects of Starvation

Individuals who suffer from anorexia nervosa are basically starving themselves–if not to death, then as close as they can get to it. Anorexia nervosa has the highest death rate of any mental illness. Between 5% and 20% of people who develop the disease eventually die from it. The longer the individual has it, the more likely they will die from it. Even for those who survive, the disorder can damage almost every body system.

Because a principle symptom of anorexia is denial–many patients don't understand that their actions are directly contributing to declining health–it can be useful to educate the patient on the actual, measurable effects of starvation on the human body. It's also important for health care providers to know the timeline of damage done to the body by starvation, whether self-imposed or brought upon by economic calamity.

The body needs food to survive, and can't last long without it.

When food intake ceases–or is chronically insufficient, as in anorexia nervosa–the body enters the starvation response, a state in which the body is responding to prolonged periods of low energy intake levels. During short periods of energy abstinence, the human body will burn primarily free fatty acids from body fat stores, along with small amounts of muscle tissue to provide required glucose for the brain.

In the absence of dietary sugars and carbohydrates, glucose is obtained from the breakdown of stored glycogen. Glycogen is a readily accessible storage form of glucose, stored in notable quantities in the liver and in small quantities in the muscles.

When the glycogen reserve is depleted, glucose can be obtained from the breakdown of fats from adipose tissue. Fats are broken down into glycerol and free fatty acids, with the glycerol being utilized in the liver as a substrate for gluconeogenesis.

When even the glycerol reserves are depleted, or sooner, the liver will start producing ketone bodies. Ketone bodies are short-chain derivatives of fatty acids, which, since they are capable of crossing the blood–brain barrier, can be used by the brain as an alternative metabolic fuel. Fatty acids can be used directly as an energy source by most tissues in the body.

As starvation progresses, the cells in the body begin to break down protein. This releases amino acids into the bloodstream, which can be converted into glucose by the liver. Since much of our muscle mass is protein, this phenomenon is responsible for the wasting away of muscle mass seen in starvation.

The loss of body protein affects the function of important organs, and death results, even if there are still fat reserves left unused. (In a leaner person, the fat reserves are depleted earlier, the protein depletion occurs sooner, and therefore death occurs sooner.) As the body loses muscle mass, it loses heart muscle at a preferential rate, so the heart gets smaller and weaker. It gets worse at increasing your circulation in response to exercise, and the pulse and blood pressure get lower. The cardiac tolls are acute and significant, and set in quickly. Heart damage is the most common reason for hospitalization in people with anorexia.

The ultimate cause of death is often cardiac arrhythmia or cardiac arrest brought on by tissue degradation and electrolyte imbalances. Autophagy may occur, in which cells cannibalize critical molecules to produce amino acids for gluconeogenesis. This process distorts the structure of the cells, and a common cause of death in starvation is due to diaphragm failure from prolonged autophagy.

Signs and Symptoms

Early symptoms of starvation include impulsivity, irritability, and hyperactivity. Atrophy (wasting away) of the stomach weakens the perception of hunger, since the perception is controlled by the percentage of the stomach that is empty.

Vitamin deficiency is a common result of starvation, often leading to anemia, beriberi, pellagra, and scurvy. These diseases collectively can also cause diarrhea, skin rashes, edema, and heart failure. Individuals are often irritable and lethargic as a result.

About half of all anorexics have low white-blood-cell counts, and about a third are anemic. Both conditions can lower the immune system's resistance to disease, leaving a person vulnerable to infections.

The brain actually shrinks due to lack of nutrition. The skeletal system is damaged, especially if the anorexia occurs in adolescents before the bones are fully developed. Nearly 90% of women with anorexia experience osteopenia (loss of bone calcium) and 40% have osteoporosis (more advanced loss of bone density). This bone loss is usually permanent.

If accompanied by severe dehydration, all movements become painful due to muscle atrophy and dry, cracked skin that is caused by dehydration. With a weakened body, diseases are commonplace. Fungi, for example, often grow under the esophagus, making swallowing painful.

The energy deficiency inherent in starvation causes fatigue and renders the victim more apathetic over time. As the starving person becomes too weak to move or even eat, their interaction with the surrounding world diminishes. In females, menstruation ceases when the body fat percentage is too low to support a fetus. This is not uncommon in patients with anorexia nervosa, and the return of menses is one sign that the patient is recovering.

While there's insufficient scientific data on exactly how long people can live without food, data suggests that in adults complete starvation leads to death within eight to twelve weeks of total food deprivation. (If water is withheld, a person will generally die within ten days.) Starvation begins when an individual has lost about 30% of their normal body weight. Once the loss reaches 40%, death is almost inevitable. Therefore, if an adult has a baseline body weight of 140 pounds, once they reach eighty pounds they're in serious risk of death.

A Healthy Relationship to Food

In order to develop a healthy relationship to food it is important to understand the critical role of food in nourishing the body and sustaining life, as well as how the brain is affected when nutrition is lacking and the body goes into starvation mode without energy to think clearly. Journaling about food, feelings and stresses surrounding eating are usually required as part of nutritional counseling and other therapies. It can be helpful not only in learning to express inner feelings, but also later in treatment when rereading journal entries can be very helpful to the patient in reviewing their progress and anchoring the gains that they have made in their struggles with food.

Eating disordered patients are also taught about genetics and how heredity plays a large role in body shape and in the range of caloric intake their body requires. Armed with this information, the patient is retrained to see food not as "good" or "bad" but as options that offer different kinds of energy for the body to do its work. Patients have to be trained to understand the feelings of hunger and fullness. They have to change how they approach food. This is a substantial task but it is done in combination with other therapy so what might not work alone, works together to help each person find a new way to frame the fuel they need for life. Each client is helped to see the reality of their eating disorder and what it has done to them.

Dr. James Greenblatt, a licensed psychiatrist and the chief medical officer of Walden Behavioral Care in Massachusetts, wrote a book called *Answers to Anorexia: A Breakthrough Nutritional Treatment That is Saving Lives.* He explains that the importance of good nutrition and balanced meals creates a positive atmosphere for recovery. He feels that the role food plays in preventing a setback is in part due to the relief of symptoms. Food is nourishment to the brain, and the resulting better health motivates many into effective participation in their therapy. If the patient is more involved in therapy, he or she will be more apt to change their own personal habits and family habits.

Greenblatt points out that those who suffer from eating disorders often present with major deficits in zinc, vitamin B-12, and amino acid tryptophan, which contribute to anxiety. In the case of zinc deficits, it is not good enough to simply eat foods with zinc but it must be consumed with foods that help the body absorb the zinc. Patients who learn this and are able to see how eating healthy food is a beginning toward gaining control of their anxiety and their eating disorder have taken a huge step towards healing.

Those patients who are vegetarians must understand how to get the minerals and vitamins they need in various ways. Greenblatt developed a five-point plan for anorexia patients: Optimize zinc levels, evaluate deficient digestive enzymes and the flora in the gut, correct underlying nutritional deficiencies – especially B vitamins and essential fatty acids, check for celiac disease and gluten or other allergies, and lastly get a brain scan to identify which medications might be effective. He also recommends each patient have referenced-electroencephalogram (rEEG) to measure brainwaves. He notes that this can be used to compare profiles of other similar-aged patients to take the guesswork out of prescribing drug or drug combinations.

Nutritional Counseling

A large problem faced by nutritional therapists is that many people; don't understand how to eat balanced diets, so those who suffer from eating disorders require a complete education in this area. Nutritional counseling faces the task of helping each patient toward a medical stability with healthy food, normalizing eating behaviors and building positive relationship with food. Those with eating disorders often have fears of what they call their forbidden food lists, believe myths about certain foods and have lost the ability to acknowledge hunger. Though for some, feeling hunger became a reward for not eating.

In her book *Eating Disorders,* Pamela Keel writes about the need to spend a lot of time in nutritional therapy on the relationship between eating, the body's use of and need for energy and what an appropriate weight is in order to prepare them to take charge of their eating, shopping for food and food preparation. The misconception by many who suffer from eating disorders is that they have to burn off every calorie they eat with exercise. What they don't consider is the calories or energy it takes just to keep the body running. Nutritionists do much more than help patients balance a diet. They have to educate them about how food is required to keep their heart beating. Anyone who restricts their diet is starving their body from the nutrition and calories it takes to simply function. Reparation will take a long time but each person must begin with balancing their food intake and eating the right number of calories immediately upon starting treatment and even with that, there may be some damage that is irreversible.

Someone who is learning how to eat properly again, or maybe for the first time in their life, needs to understand that the mind is only as healthy as the body. Building the mind back means giving back more resources both psychological and behavioral that can be used to make and keep them strong for those times when the old feelings and thoughts try to come back, set up rules and take over again. It is a little like going on diets to lose weight. Thousands of new books are written on the subject, and new fad diets appear daily. People buy into each new thing that goes around. Over the years some people have gone through so many diets and yet have not lost the weight they intended to lose. One might consider the reason for this is that these diets just don't work. It is not hard to understand how habitual thinking can be so difficult to change.

A better way for all people to develop healthy bodies is not to "diet" (meaning restricting food) but to balance what is eaten and be aware of how different foods react in your body. Too much is said about food that just isn't true and people who crave thinness are vulnerable to believing anything.

Dr. Angela Doyle on the Maudsley Parents website blogs about an adolescent female who recovered her weight with the Maudsley Family Therapy procedures and was released to begin to take charge of her own eating. She immediately lost weight, so her parents took the control of her eating back.

After regaining the weight, the counselor again advised they give her control again. And again the same thing happened.

Dr. Doyle recommend that they remember that each person will have an individual recovery rate and that with their daughter it might work better to put her in charge of a snack and adding back in each meal over more time instead of all at once. She also reminded the parents that their daughter still needed to continue therapy for the underlying anxiety issues that had initially pushed her into such "coping measures."

Development of a nutritionally balanced eating habit takes time and effort for the eating disordered individual and their support system. It can require taking control for lengths of time that cannot be predicted. Each person is different in the way they think, feel, and respond to life. The success for regaining control with ED appears to be a multifaceted approach. It requires controlling the food the person will eat, requiring them to eat, getting them involved with cognitive and behavioral therapy and nutritional counseling to educate about the relationship between food and the body. It has to become personal to each individual.

Simply forcing someone to eat without giving them therapy to retrain the brain and education about how unhealthy eating habits affect the brain and the body won't move them toward healthy thinking and healthy eating. It all comes down to disruption of the fixations of the brain. To get this release, the patient has to find a new way to deal with anxiety and depression in order to learn to develop new ways to eating. It requires years of cognitive, behavioral, nutritional and possibly many other kinds of therapy to retrain thinking and behaviors. Nutrition, behaviors, physical and mental health and brain processing are cyclical in nature and very deeply connected. You cannot have good health in any of these areas if even one part is disrupted or compromised in some way. A whole-body approach is the best way to support a person with an eating disorder because the whole person is involved, physically, psychologically, and emotionally.

CHAPTER 12

Preventing and Recovering from Eating Disorders

Jeremy Gillitzer was born in St. Paul, Minnesota, on August 23, 1971. His biological dad abandoned him, and his mother, who worked at a department store, married a carpenter, who dutifully adopted Jeremy.

Jeremy was a pudgy kid, still carrying his baby fat, and his weight was a frequent target for his stepfather's ire. "He'd always say I was fat, or needed to lose weight," Jeremy told writer Kevin Hoffman in the Minneapolis-St.Paul online paper City Pages.

If that wasn't enough, Jeremy was going through puberty and confronting the fact that he was gay. The very thought of it horrified him. He could only imagine how his stepdad would react.

Then, when he was twelve, Jeremy discovered a solution to both problems: starvation.

"It serves two purposes," Jeremy said. "It serves a very applied purpose in that if you're doing the behaviors, you don't have time to think about being gay. And also being malnourished, you don't feel sexual, so you don't have to worry about being gay or straight."

Soon, Jeremy was suffering advanced symptoms of starvation. He was sensitive to cold and had grown a fine coat of body hair. He saw a doctor in November 1983 who took one look at the 85-pound boy and diagnosed him with anorexia nervosa.

A month later, after losing nine more pounds, Jeremy entered Children's Hospital of St. Paul. "Jeremy is a 12-year-old boy admitted for evaluation and treatment of anorexia nervosa," reads the December 15, 1983 evaluation. "He is somewhat irritable and is having difficulty concentrating on his schoolwork. He is substantially small for his age."

As Jeremy grew older, he became proficient at vomiting up everything and anything he had eaten. He cycled through treatment centers, devising ever more elaborate ways to hide his vomit from the staff. Sent to a particularly strict hospital, he was force-fed and forbidden from visiting the toilet after meals. "I'd do things to get around them, like throw up in big cups and then hide them, both in the day room and in my room. I would throw up in the washing machine and run it through the rinse cycle–I did that once, I shouldn't say I did that regularly. But it's amazing what you'll do."

After a period of hospitalization, he was released and he got his own apartment. And then something amazing happened: Jeremy got better. At age twenty-one, he came out of the closet. Gradually, he stopped binging and purging. Freed of his symptoms, Jeremy enrolled at the University of Minnesota–this time as a student rather than a patient. He pursued his interest in political science, becoming so convinced that he would one day run for office that he had "Jeremy's Campaign for Congress" emblazoned on his checks.

He transformed his body. After applying the same rigor to bodybuilding that he'd used in starving himself, the once-emaciated man showed off bulging pecs and six-pack abs. He found work as a male model and even had a few small cameos in movies. In a bid to secure more work, he stepped up his exercise routine, hitting the gym for up to five hours a day.

In 2004, everything fell apart. Jeremy's relationship with his first and only long-term boyfriend ended in a torrent of jealousy and hurt feelings. Then his mother fell seriously ill. Two car accidents within a month pushed him over the edge.

Overwhelmed, Jeremy returned to the comfort of his old routine. He was soon deep in the throes of his old eating disorder. After police stormed his house after concerned a family member called to report that Jeremy was a threat to himself, he was involuntarily committed to a hospital.

In 2010, unable to overcome his inner struggle with his eating disorder, he died. He weighed sixty-six pounds.

The tragedy of Jeremy Gillitzer is that he knew exactly what his disease was. He could describe it and talk about it. But in his mind, it was a force he could not resist. His determination to starve himself was as much a part of him as breathing.

Prevention and Recovery

No one sees an eating disorder coming. It moves into a life slowly, changing patterns, of not just eating, but of response behaviors to all things. Because eating disorders are not about the food, but about trying to gain control over life where intense anxiety is taking place, and because those anxieties often start in childhood or after some trauma, it becomes very important for adults to know how anxiety, tension and obsessive-compulsive behavior can go very wrong, very quickly if not dealt with appropriately.

Preventing an eating disorder is most often hindered by ignorance and an inability to admit there are issues. Ignorance comes from a lack of understanding the psychological needs of children and since most eating disorders are based in emotional traumas in childhood, it becomes urgent that parents attain this knowledge in some way. Children can be severely and adversely affected by stresses that adults handle well. Because children are still developing their emotional stability, resilience, and their ability to trust others, you have to consider how disruptions in life can affect the delicacy of the mind of a child.

There are three kinds of stress to consider. Positive, or "normal,: stress is encountered when a child gets a new caregiver, the first day of school, being in the car during a fender-bender, or getting rain when the plans include going to the zoo or a birthday party in the park. This stress is positive because it can be faced, and responded to by a child with an adult for support and done so, for the most part, in a short period of time. If a child cannot handle this so-called "normal positive stress" with adult support, then the child may suffer from a most severe anxiety disorder that requires immediate assessment by professionals.

The second kind of stress is called "tolerable stress." It includes more severe stress like the loss of someone they knew and loved, a difficult personal injury, or a natural disaster that puts the entire family into stress.

The final classification of stress is "toxic stress." Toxic stress is a very negative experience, especially for a child. It can occur if the stress extends over long periods, is frequent or severe. Abuse, neglect, being around adults who are mentally ill, and living in distressing conditions like orphanages where caregivers come and go and little bonding with any one individual takes place are included in this category. Children who are exposed to this, without any relief from competent adult support, are at risk for disruption of development of the brain, organs, and related issues like cognitive impairment.

The negative effects of stress can be reversed if they are targeted effectively and early. Children need adults who are trustworthy, caring and can support them through stressful situations. An intervention that takes place in the life of a child who lives in an environment of toxic stress, to be successful, requires adults who are committed to bonding relationships with that child for a lifetime. The requirement is great but the results are great as well.

Children were meant to live in groups where adult support protects them, allows them to grow naturally, and provides trusting and loving relationships.

But even children from "good" homes can confront stress that is not recognized as more than tolerable or that might be tolerable for one child but not for another. Given that every person develops at different speeds, it is a mistake to think all children, even in the same family, will deal with all stress alike. The lines between positive, tolerable and toxic stress are not easily drawn and often overlap.

If you have taken on the responsibility to raise children in today's world you cannot raise them like you were raised. Things are different. Like it or not, your children will confront many of the same issues you did as a child but they will also confront issues that you never dreamed possible. Children are exposed to violence, danger, decisions, and experiences that once would have been uncommon or even unknown only one generation ago.

Parents cannot blindly allow children to live as though they were adults. Children need and want boundaries and clear direction. Parents must be observant, act in adult ways, and be in charge of protecting their children. That doesn't mean you never allow stress to enter your child's life. That positive stress and tolerable stress your children experience does not mean you are not needed to stand with them as they go through the stress. Children will need support, encouragement and for those they need to have a trusting relationship with their parents.

Leaving children to figure out the world on their own without a supportive and trusting adult relationship is a basis for psychological problems of many kinds. What is seen as positive or tolerable stress, faced without parental support that is strong can turn into toxic stress. If a child is left at a daycare on the first day by an adult they have not learned to trust, in the arms of an adult they don't know at all, tolerable stress could become toxic stress.

If the treatment exercises for ED individuals are examined, they might be considered as some of the same exercises you would use to show children how to deal with stress. For example, having an image of a safe calm place in your mind so you have a "mental safe place" that you can go anytime, anywhere. Identifying the emotions of others and yourself and understanding the sensations felt in your body, development of activities that are soothing like listening to music, taking a walk or reading, remembering good experiences, using cue words to trigger calmness such as swimming, beach, self-talk with positive words, and finding spiritual connections and positive relationships with others. In the day when children could run free around a small town where everyone could be trusted, or before the Internet and when television content was more controlled and family friendly, parents didn't need to parent about how to deal with stress in such direct ways. Today it is a different story.

Today, you don't know if you can trust the school bus driver, the teacher, the neighbor, or the parents of your children's friends. You cannot however hover so much that your children are unable to develop a natural resilience to positive and tolerable stress. Parents have to be aware, observant, and smart. Each parent will have to find a balance between allowing some independence with children and protecting their children. There is no rule. Knowing how to achieve this balance must be figured out as you experience parenthood and you will make mistakes. The key is to recognize whether those mistakes are too protective or not supportive enough, and to make changes accordingly. Don't be apologetic for taking charge of the way you raise your children. If you are doing what is emotionally, physically and cognitively necessary for healthy growth in all ways then you need to stand strong. Your parenting will develop within your beliefs and values and as you experience life with children, those things may change slightly because parenting is a learning experience.

There are several models and variation of those models for disease prevention through educational programs in schools or other organized centers.

One is based on identification of risk factors and how they might be modified, along with development of body image.

Another is to identify risk factors that are based in the underlying mental illness factors like anxiety or depression and to develop healthier thinking.

A third model emphasizes protective factors rather than risk factors. This is often called a "health promotional paradigm." It ignores body image and eating and instead educated youth and communities of individuals about the value of differences and being accepting of those differences in others as well as themselves.

Still another model is empowerment and relationships methods. This method seeks to focus on the skills and creative factors of girls, and having diversity of relationships that focus on the positive aspects of others to build an acceptance of self. Different programs for prevention, especially among girls, teaches them how to be media literate, develop self-esteem. Prevention has shown limited success over time. The ability of such programs to reduce dieting, address underlying mental illness risk factors and to create a long-term change in behaviors is a concern.

In recovery from an eating disorder, an individual has to find their place again in a world that is not surrounded by food and control issues. For this to happen most treatment involves imagining what life would be like and often journaling about life beyond the walls that have contained them for so long. Learning how to cope in different and more positive ways must be practiced over time. The eating disordered individual who has suffered a long time will fear they cannot manage without the supports of treatment. Treatment should allow for a gradual release to give each person a chance to learn how to stand on his or her own feet, to find confidence and to practice making new decisions, new thinking processes and new habits.

Mortality from eating disorders, once cited "starvation" or "malnutrition" as the primary cause of death, but that has changed to "suicide." The biggest indicators of death from eating disorders are low weight combined with poor psychosocial functions and alcohol use due to the chance of alcohol poisoning and low weight.

Recovery rates from severe eating disorder have increased over time. According to a blog by Kathleen Franco at the Cleveland Clinic Foundation (2012), about one-third of eating disordered patients diagnosed and treated recover from eating disorders completely, about a third recover back to the beginning of their eating disorder, and a third are unable to make improvements.

Recovery takes a big commitment from the individual and from his support system, and can take many years. It requires a change in thought and behavior. It is a process that is unique to the individual. It involves the development of coping strategies that are healthy and a change in thought patterns. For many eating disordered patients, recovery is unimaginable and it takes treatment to help it become a reality. There are stages of recovery. The stages take the patient through uncomfortable feelings, frustrations, and possible relapses. Recovery will involve not just the individual but their family and friends. Challenges are still there for those who have suffered with eating disorders but with time, support and practice they can be overcome. The patient has to learn to deal with the underlying issues and triggers that they will confront.

Crossover Eating Disorders

Development of a crossover ED is common during recovery. That means moving from one form to another, like from anorexia nervosa to binging and purging. In her book, *Eating Disorders*, Greene offers a set of guidelines to use in recovery. She promotes protecting yourself from inappropriate comments from others by setting boundaries on what you divulge, be ready to answer questions directly and truthfully about eating disorders, know a few resources you can offer to those who inquire for help, know your triggers and don't go into the details about your disorder that you should not dwell on or that may perpetuate your illness and interrupt your recovery, allow yourself to share general medical and negative cognitive and social consequences but also the hope in recovery, and lastly emphasize that early intervention and treatment is very important.

Life in recovery requires a slower pace, time to stop and consider choices and attention to good health. It does not mean no more therapy or check-ups for physical and mental health. It is a continuation of learning how to cope with stress, developing healthy relationships and supports, and being very aware of feelings and emotions. Some consider life in recovery like those with other addictions. Recovery is a lifelong quest and requires mindful attention.

Resources that Focus on Eating Disorders

Today the internet is probably the first place a person would look to find resources for an eating disorder. The following resources are readily available online and are designed to address he needs of professionals working with eating disorders, as well as individuals and their families who are struggling with disordered eating.

The National Eating Disorders Association (NEDA)

The National Eating Disorders Association (NEDA) is a tax-exempt, non-profit organization in the United States that advocates for and supports those affected with eating disorders, including their support systems and families. NEDA works for prevention and improved treatment and research. It was founded in 2001 when the Eating Disorders Awareness & Prevention (EDAP) and the Anorexia Bulimia Association (AABA) combined. Previously, the National Eating Disorder Organization (NEDO) and the Anorexia Nervosa & Related Disorders (ANRED) had combined with AABA and NEDO. Their shared resources are now available through NEDA which provides a wealth of information in one place. This organization has a founder's council, research advisory council, prevention advisory council, ambassador council, a junior board, partners, sustaining sponsors and a network of other organizations who are dedicated to the cause. The strength of this organization is advocacy role in the battle against eating disorders.

NEDA offers a toolkit for parents that gives answers to questions that parents routinely seek when they need information to help a child with eating disorders. It explains about the various disorders, treatments, what represents an emergency and how to deal with school issues when their child is too ill to attend. In addition to the parent toolkit, they offer a separate toolkit for teachers and coaches because those who work with children and adolescents on a regular basis can help identify those at risk. Not only does NEDA offer the toolkits, they also publish magazines on a regular basis that focus on different eating disorder issues, and they offer videos and webinars. They also offer assistance concerning insurance systems and how individuals can secure coverage for individuals and families.

Treatment Centers

There are many centers for treatment and support. In the book, *Maintaining Recovery from Eating Disorders*, Naomi Feignbaum shares the personal recovery stories of many individuals who have gone through treatment and are recovering. The stories provide hope for others and explain how once the eating is under control, underlying issues can be dealt with. Those who told of their experiences talked of relationships, spirituality and trauma. They discussed their own unique challenges and how they now cope with life in recovery. The eating disordered individuals in this book discuss how to make transitions from treatment centers back into the real world, how to use the treatment teams in their out-patient support and how to prepare for the journey they face. In sharing their lives with Feignbaum, they opened up about celebrating the person they really are, confronting triggers and the success of treating food as medicine for good health. Participating in creative activities, and healthy relationships and connecting with their spiritual side are common themes.

This author points out that when struggles arise during recovery, being able to read about the successes of other and how they worked through challenges can be very helpful. She also sees this book as providing support and hope to families and friends of the ED person. "Listening" to these emotional vignettes of the lives of those who share their personal experiences in recovery, provides a healthy and supportive text for others in recovery with a focus on new skills, habits, and relationships.

American Dietetic Association

Other resources come from the American Dietetic Association, whose goal is to help the public benefit from a healthy lifestyle and healthy eating. They focus on obesity in children, aging, maintenance of a sustainable and nutritious food supply, nutrigenomics, integrative medicine and alternative medicines. They are supported by the Academy for Eating Disorders, National Women's Health Information Center and the Female Athlete Triad, among others.

Eating Disorders Books and Resources

Greene, in her book, "Eating Disorders," at the end of each chapter, lists other helpful books to read, videos to watch and associations that provide information, support, professionals who can help deal with an eating disorder.

She also lists events that raise money, and lists of contacts where eating disordered individuals can find ways to get involved with others, as well as ways to find others who are willing to take action to get involved with the eating disordered individual.

Eating Disorders Resource Catalogue

The Eating Disorders Resource Catalogue and website is another place that offers an abundance of information and they show concern for all categories of gender, race and culture. Tom Wooldridge, Psy.D., in one of his posts discusses working with males who are diagnosed with anorexia nervosa. He describes the four stages that work best with males: engagement, alliance building, diagnosis, and ongoing treatment processes. He gives very good information about males and eating disorders and, like other professionals who write posts, he has written a couple of books. Wooldridge emphasizes an integrative treatment program that has a focus on underlying conditions and not on symptoms or the eating disorder itself.

Thought Catalogue

Another great resource is an online magazine called Thought Catalogue. It boasts over thirty million readers per month, and provides a platform for writers, new and experienced, to express themselves about eating disorders. It encourages creativity and artistic expressions through the written word. It allows those who have experienced eating disorders themselves, or those who have experienced eating disorders within their families, with friends or those who work with ED individuals to write and publish. It offers a broad array of personal stories that provide support, hope and understanding, and a place to express deep feelings.

World Eating Disorders

A website call World Eating Disorders Action Day lists helplines, organizations and places to contact help and information about eating disorders from over fifteen different countries. Their listings do no imply endorsement, but they do actively recruit the nomination of other useful sources of information or treatment in support of their role as a clearinghouse of resources within the field.

Innerthought

In a website called "innerthought," licensed therapists Marsea Marcus and Andrea Wachter, write books, some for children, and offer audio and Skype classes in support of those with eating disorders. They use humor and personal experiences to help people see the truth about diets and weight. Their focus is on the thought processes of ED individuals, and they are located in Northern California where they have identified a wide range of eating disorder resources within their region.

Canped.com

Canped.com is a website created by Dr. Wendy Spettigue and Dr. Mark Norris as a tool to support parents, caregivers and health care providers for youth that may have eating disorders. They offer books and links but also free Power Point modules that are informative and easy to follow.

Abigail Natenshon

Abigail Natenshon is a psychotherapist with forty-five years of experience working with eating disorders. She offers support for parents, patients, health professionals and help for prevention. Her website, called Abigail Natenshon's Treating Eating Disorders, offers everything from information, books, links, and she offers to team up with other eating disorder therapists on their cases.

RECOMMENDED RESOURCES

American Psychiatric Association, & American Psychiatric Association. (2013). *Diagnostic and statistical manual of mental disorders: DSM-5*. Washington, DC: American Psychiatric Association.

Choate, L. H. (2013). *Eating Disorders and Obesity A Counselor's Guide to Prevention and Treatment*. Alexandria, VA: American Counseling Association.

Koenig, K. R. (2007). *The food & feelings workbook: A full course meal on emotional health*. Carlsbad, CA: Gürze Books.

Rowell, K., McGlothlin, J., & Morris, S. E. (2015). *Helping your child with extreme picky eating: A step-by-step guide for overcoming selective eating, food aversion, and feeding disorders*. Oakland, CA: New Harbinger Publications, Inc.

REFERENCES

American Psychiatric Association, (2000). Practice guidelines for the treatment of patients with eating disorders. *Am J Psychiatry.* 2000;(Suppl 1):157. 1.

Austin, S. Bryn, (2004). Sexual Orientation, Weight Concerns, and Eating-Disordered Behaviors in Adolescent Girls and Boys. *Journal of the American Academy of Child & Adolescent Psychiatry.* V43.

Aviram, Adi; Westra, Henny A.; Constantino, Michael J.; Antony, & Martin M., (2016). *Journal of Consulting and Clinical Psychology.* Vol 84(9), Sep 2016, 783-794. http://dx.doi.org/10.1037/ccp0000100

Balch, Katheryn, March 22, 2011. Blog Title: When Pregnancy and Eating Disorders Mix. http://abcnews.go.com/Health/WomensHealth/pregorexia-pregnancy-eating-disorders-mix/story?id=13143285

Bandini E[1], Fisher AD, Castellini G, Lo Sauro C, Lelli L, Meriggiola MC, Casale H, Benni L, Ferruccio N, Faravelli C, Dettore D, Maggi M, & Ricca V. (2013) *Journal of Sexual Medicine.* 2013 Apr;10(4):1012-23. doi: 10.1111/jsm.12062. Epub 2013 Jan 24.

Birch, L., Fisher, J., & Krahnstoever, K. (2013). Learning to overeat: maternal use of restrictive feeding practices promotes girls' eating in the absence of hunger. *American Journal of Clinical Nutrition.* Accessed online 30 Nov 2016 http://ajcn.nutrition.org/content/78/2/215.abstract#aff-1

Bischoff-Grethe, A., McCurdy, D., Grenesko-Stevens, E., Irvine, L., Wagner, A., Yau W. Y., et al. (2013). Altered brain response to reward and punishment in adolescents with anorexia nervosa. *Psychiatry Research*, 214, 331–340. doi: 10.1016/j.pscychresns. 2013.07.004

Brewerton, T. (2004). Pharmacotherapy for Patients With Eating Disorders. *Psychiatric Times*, May 01, 2004.

Brown, T.A. & Keel, P.K. (2012). The impact of relationships in the association between sexual orientation and disordered eating in men. *International Journal of Eating Disorders*, 2012;45:792-799.

Bruch, H. (1973). *Eating Disorders: Obesity, anorexia nervosa and the person within.* New York, Basic Books.

Bulik, Cynthia M. (2013). The challenges of treating anorexia nervosa. *The Lancet*, 14 October 2013.

Cloninger, C.R., Svrakic, D.M., & Przbeck, T.R. (1993). A psychobiological model of temperament and character. *Archives of General Psychiatry*, 50, 975-900.

Dansky BS, Brewerton TD, Kilpatrick DG, O'Neil PM. (1997). The National Women's Study: relationship of victimization and posttraumatic stress disorder to bulimia nervosa. *International Journal of Eating Disorders.* 1997;21(3):213-228.

Feigenbaum, N. (2012). *Maintaining Recovery from Eating Disorders.* Philadelphia, PA; Jessica Kingsley Publishers.

Feldman, M.B., & Meyer, I.H. (2007). Childhood abuse and eating disorders in gay and bisexual men. *International Journal of Eating Disorders*, 40(5), 418-423.

Feldman, M.B., & Meyer, I.H. (2007). Eating Disorders in Diverse Lesbian, Gay, and Bisexual Populations. *International Journal of Eating Disorders*, 40(3): 218–226.

Fitzgibbon, M. L., Spring B., Avellone, M. E., Blackman, L.R., Pingitore, R., & Stolley, M. R., (1998). Correlates of binge eating in Hispanic, black and white women. *International Journal of Eating Disorders,* 24,43-52.

Fluoxetine Bulimia Nervosa Collaborative Study Group (1992). Fluoxetine in the treatment of bulimia nervosa. A multicenter, placebo-controlled, double-blind trial. *Arch Gen Psychiatry.* 1992;49:139.

Golden, N., Katzman, D., Kreipe, R., et al. (2003). Eating disorders in adolescents: Position paper of the Society for Adolescent Medicine. *J Adolesc Health.* 2003;33:496.

Gorla, K. & Mathews, M. (2005). Pharmacological Treatment of Eating Disorder. *Psychiatry (Edgmont).* 2005 Jun; 2(6): 43–48.

Greene, J.R. (2014). *Eating Disorders.* New York, NY; Rowman & Littlefield.

Grilo, CM, Masheb, RM, & Wilson, GT,J. (2001). A comparison of different methods for assessing the features of eating disorders in patients with binge eating disorder. *Journal of Consulting and Clinical Psychology.* 2001 Apr;69(2):317-22.

Inniss, D., Steiger, H., & Bruce, K.. (2011). Threshold and subthreshold post-traumatic stress disorder in bulimic patients: Prevalences and clinical correlates. *Eating and Weight Disorders - Studies on Anorexia, Bulimia and Obesity.* 2011;16(1):e30-6.

Johnson, Marlys. (2000). *Understanding Exercise Addiction.* The Rosen Publishing Company, Inc. New York.

Judd, Sandra J. (2011). *Eating Disorders Sourcebook* (3rd ed.). Detroit, MI. Omnigraphics, Inc.

Kaye WH, Wagner A, Fudge JL, & Paulus M. (2011).Neurocircuity of eating disorders. *Current Topics in Behavioral Neurosciences.* 2011;6:37-57.

Kaye W. (2008) Neurobiology of anorexia and bulimia nervosa. *Physiology & Behavior.* 94(1):121-135.

Keel, P.K. (2009). *Eating Disorders.* Upper Saddle River, New Jersey; Pearson Education, Inc.

Keel, P.K. & Forney, J. (2103). Psychosocial risk factors for eating disorders. *International Journal of Eating*, Vol 46(5), Jul 2013, 433-439.

Kenney, L. & Walsh, B. T. (2013). Avoidant/Restrictive Food Intake Disorder (ARFID). *Eating Disorders Review*, May/June Volume 24, Number 3.

Kracke, E. & Tosh, A.(2014). Treatment of anorexia nervosa with long-term risperidone in an outpatient setting: case study. *SpringerPlus*. 20143:706. DOI: 10.1186/2193-1801-3-706

Kristeller, J. & Hallett, C.B. (1999). An Exploratory Study of a Meditation-Based Intervention for Binge Eating Disorder. *Journal of Health Psychology*. Vol 4 (3). 357-363.

Lemberg, R. & Phillips, J. (1989), The impact of pregnancy on anorexia nervosa and bulimia. *Int. J. Eat. Disord.*, 8: 285–295. doi:10.1002/1098-108X(198905)8:3<285::AID-EAT2260080304>3.0.CO;2-P

Lewis, L. & le Grange, D. (1994), The experience and impact of pregnancy in bulimia nervosa: A series of case studies. *Eur. Eat. Disorders Rev.*, 2: 93–105. doi:10.1002/erv.2400020205.

Mahler, P.S., & Anderson A.E. (1999). *Eating Disorders; A Guide to Medical Care and Complications* (2nd ed.). Baltimore, MD; The John Hopkins University Press

Matusek, Anne & O'Dougherty, Margaret. (2010). Ethical Dilemmas in Treating Clients with Eating Disorders: A Review and Application of an Integrative Ethical Decision-making Model. Jill Wright Department of Psychology, Miami University, OH, USA. Published online 30 July 2010 in Wiley Online Library (wileyonlinelibrary.com) DOI:

Mazzeo, S. & Bulik, C. (2009). Environmental and genetic risk factors for eating disorders: What the clinician needs to know. *Child and Adolescent Psychiatric Clinics of North America*. Jan; 18(1): 67–82.

Michigan State University. (2007, May 12). Genetic Risk Factors For Eating Disorders Discovered. *ScienceDaily*. Retrieved November 30, 2016 from www.sciencedaily.com/releases/2007/05/070511150158.htm

Mintz, L. B., & Betz, N. E. (1988). Prevalence and correlates of eating disordered behaviors among undergraduate women. *Journal of Counseling Psychology*, 35, 463- 471. R

Nowakowski, M., McFarlane, T. & Cassin, S. (2013). Alexithymia and eating disorders: a critical review of the literature. *Journal of Eating Disorders*, 1:21. DOI: 10.1186/2050-2974-1-21.

Nunn, K., Frampton, I., Gordon, I., & Lask, B. (2008). The fault is not in her parents but in her insula—A neurobiological hypothesis of anorexia nervosa. *European Eating Disorders Review*, 16, 355–360. doi: 10.1002/erv.890

Pope, H.G. Jr., Gruber, A.J, Choi, P., Olivardia, R., & Borowiecki, J. (1999). Evolving ideals of male body image as seen through action toys. *International Journal of Eating Disorders*, 26, 65-72

Reyes-Rodriguez, M., Von Holle, A,, & Ulman, T., et al. (2011). Posttraumatic stress disorder in anorexia nervosa. *Psychosomatic Medicine*. 2011;73(6):491-497.

Rieger, E., Touyz, S.W., Swain, T., & Beumont, P.J.(2001). Cross-cultural research on anorexia nervosa: Assumptions regarding the role of body weight. *International Journal of Eating Disorders*, 29, 205-215.

Rudd, N. A., Davis, L, & Winkle, P. (2010). Eating disorder causes, The Ohio State University Body Image Health Task Force, http://ehe.osu.edu/cs/bitf/.

Share, T. L. & Mintz, L.B. (2002). Differences between lesbians and heterosexual women in disordered eating and related attitudes. *Journal of Homosexuality*, 2002;4:89-106.

Simon, E. J. & Hiller, J M. (1978). The Opiate Receptors. *Annual Review of Pharmacology and Toxicology*. Vol. 18: 371-394 (Volume publication date April 1978). DOI: 10.1146/annurev.pa.18.040178.002103

Small, Arnold C. (1984) The Contribution of Psychodiagnostic Test Results Toward Understanding Anorexia Nervosa. *Journal of International Eating Disorders*. Vol. 3, No.2, 1984 winter.

Striegel-Moore, R. H., Schreiber, G. B., Lo, A., Crawford, P., Obarzanek, R., & Rodin, J. (2000). Eating disorder symptoms in a cohort of 11-16 year old Black and White girls: The NHLBI Growth and Health Study. *International Journal of Eating Disorders*, 27, 49-66.

Thornton, L.M, Mazzeo, S.E., & Bulik, CM. (2011). The heritability of eating disorders: methods and current findings. *Current Topics in Behavioral Neurosciences*. 2011;6:141-156.

University of Maryland (2016). Eating disorders. *Medical Reference Guide*. Accessed 30 Nov. 2016 online at http://umm.edu/health/medical/reports/articles/eating-disorders.

Weltzin T.E., Fernstrom, M.H., Fernstrom, J.D., Neuberger, S.K., & Kaye, W.H. (1995). Acute tryptophan depletion and increased food intake and irritability in bulimia nervosa. *American Journal of Psychiatry*. 1995 Nov;152(11):1668-71.

Wilson, J.L., Peeble, R., & Hardy, K.K., et al. (2006). Surfing for thinness. A pilot study of pro-eating disorder Web site usage in adolescents with eating disorders. *Pediatrics*. 2006;118(6):1635-43.